READING IN AL-MUSHTARAK

READING IN AL-MUSHTARAK

A System for Democratic Socialism

Edited & Translated by
Ali Al-Assam
Majid Allawi

Original Text by
Ibrahim Allawi

an iskra book

Published by *Iskra Books* © 2024

All rights reserved.
The moral rights of the author, editors, and translators have been asserted.

Iskra Books
www.iskrabooks.org
US | England | Ireland

Iskra Books is an independent scholarly publisher—publishing original works of revolutionary theory, history, education, and art, as well as edited collections, new translations, and critical republications of older works.

ISBN-13: 979-8-3303-1322-8 (*Softcover*)

British Library Cataloguing in Publication Data
A catalogue record for this book is available from the British Library.

Library of Congress Cataloguing-in-Publication Data
A catalog record for this book is available from the Library of Congress

Cover design by Ben Stahnke
Cover painting by Dia Al-Azzawi
Editing, Proofing, and Typesetting by David Peat

CONTENTS

FRONT MATTER

A NOTE FROM THE PUBLISHER I

FOREWORD I: THE 'TWO INTEGRATIONS' OF IBRAHIM ALLAWI III
Keith Bennett

FOREWORD II: A STEP TOWARDS A PLANETARY MUSHTARAK XIII
Brandon Wolfe-Hunnicutt

EDITORS' INTRODUCTION XIX
Ali Al-Assam & Majid Allawi
— Why Al-Mushtarak? XX
— On Terminology XXII

AL-MUSHTARAK

AL-MUSHTARAK IN ISLAM 2
1. Al-Mushtarak in the Era of Ignorance [*Al-Jahiliyah*, the Pre-Islamic Era of Arabia] 3
2. Al-Mushtarak in Islam 7
3. The Fall of Islamic Communalism [*Mushtarak*] and the Emergence of Despotism 13
4. The Emergence of the Call for a New Mushtarak 20
   — Spontaneous Movements 20
   — The Emergence of the Theory of Mushtarak 26
   — The Brethren of Purity [*Ikhwan Al-Safa*] Movement 34
   — Al-Ma'arri and the Mushtarak Thought 39

AL-MUSHTARAK AND THE MODERN SOCIALIST MOVEMENT 47
1. The Nature of the State in European Capitalism 47
2. The Conditions for the Modern Socialist Revolution 51
3. What Can Replace the State? 53
4. The Mushtarak System According to the Experience of the Paris Commune 56

5. The Socialist October Revolution and the Mushtarak System 61
6. The Practical Path of Socialist Democracy in the Soviet State 63
   — Firstly, the Red Army instead of the Armed People 66
   — Secondly, Bureaucratic Administration instead of the Soviet System 69
7. Marxism and the State 72
   — And What Can We Conclude From All of This? 81

AL-MUSHTARAK AS AN ESSENTIAL COMPONENT OF DEMOCRATIC SOCIALISM 84
   — Firstly, Disbanding the Army and Replacing it with Armed People 86
   — What Replaces the Government Army? 88
   — Secondly, Democratic Freedoms 89
   — Thirdly, the National Economy in the Al-Mushtarak System 92
   — Fourthly, the Kurdish Issue 94
   — Fifthly, Arab Solidarity 95

Appendices
   I. Main Historical Events Related to Al-Mushtarak Study 101
   II. Chronology of the Split in the Iraqi Communist Party 103

Images
   — IMAGE 1.1. Dia Al-Azzawi, *Bilad al-Sawad*, 1993 II
   — IMAGE 1.2. Dr. Ibrahim Allawi XXVII
   — IMAGE 1.3. Dia Al-Azzawi, *Bilad al-Sawad*, 1994-95 XXVIII
   — IMAGE 2.1. Dia Al-Azzawi, Az Gou 105

A Note from the Publisher

AL-MUSHTARAK can be translated as "that which is shared," or "the commons." In line with the latter's more common usage in socialist history, that translation has been used throughout this work.

The original document has been lightly edited for clarity, readability, and accessibility. Footnotes will indicate sections where more extensive editing has taken place. Additional contextual information is provided throughout by footnotes beginning "**Ed. Note:**" where applicable.

Bibliographic references for Western texts have been updated with commonly-accepted English translations where possible, with some translated directly from the original Arabic text. Arabic bibliographical references were preserved from the original text. If more detailed Arabic bibliographical information is desired, please contact INFO@MUSHTAREK.ORG.

Iskra Books and the editors extend deep gratitude to Dia Al-Azzawi for the use of his painting on the cover of this book. Several of Al-Azzawi's works can be found throughout the text as well.

Image 1.1. Art by Dia Al-Azzawi. *Bilad al-Sawad*, 1993.

FOREWORD I

THE 'TWO INTEGRATIONS' OF IBRAHIM ALLAWI

KEITH BENNETT[1]

READING in *Al-Mushtarak* is an important contribution to the application and development of Marxism and needs to be approached and viewed within the context of the trajectory of scientific socialism from the nineteenth through to the twenty-first century.

Marx and Engels (as some important recent work has made increasingly clear) displayed great interest in non-western and pre-capitalist societies and in the diverse struggles for liberation of what we now call the global majority. This can be seen, inter alia, in Marx's study of the Russian commune system, exploring the potential it held for societies to transition to socialism without passing through all the horrors of the capitalist system, by 'leaping over the Caudine Forks'; Engels' study of the work of Lewis Henry Morgan in *The Origin of the Family, Private Property and the State*; Marx's journalism in the *New York Daily Tribune*, not least his articles on China; the writings of Marx on India and Engels on Afghanistan; and so on.

However, it was their detailed study of the Irish question that was pivotal in their developing understanding of the process of revolution on a worldwide scale. In April 1870, Marx wrote to Sigfrid Meyer and August Vogt:

> After studying the Irish question for many years, I have come to the conclusion that the decisive blow against the English ruling classes (and it will be

---

[1] Keith Bennett is co-editor of FRIENDS OF SOCIALIST CHINA, as well as a writer, researcher, and consultant on international relations.

decisive for the workers' movement all over the world) cannot be delivered *in England* but *only in Ireland*.[2]

This was not simply of bilateral or local significance. In May 1914, in his article, 'The Right of Nations to Self-Determination,' Lenin wrote:

> The policy of Marx and Engels on the Irish question serves as a splendid example of the attitude the proletariat of the oppressor nations should adopt towards national movements, an example which has lost none of its immense practical importance.[3]

Nevertheless, in its first organizational expression, in the First and Second Internationals, Marxism was essentially the (at least aspirant) ideology of the western proletariat, in Europe and North America.

It was the October Revolution that marked the essential first step in breaking from that paradigm. By breaking the imperialist chain at its weakest link, the revolution had triumphed and the working class had seized power in a massive country—a country with one foot still in feudalism and serfdom as much as the other was planted in capitalism and industrialization; and a country whose landmass and its numerous constituent nationalities were as much Asian as European.

Not without struggle and anguish on the part of the Bolshevik leaders—then and later—with the change of slogan from "Workers of the world unite" to "Workers and oppressed peoples of the world unite" on the part of the newly-formed Communist International, the liberation of the colonies and semi-colonies became as much a concern of the communist movement as the emancipation of the proletariat in the imperialist heartlands.

Indeed, in his last article, written in March 1923, 'Better Fewer, but Better,' Lenin went so far as to state:

> In the last analysis, the outcome of the struggle will be determined by the fact that Russia, India, China, etc., account for the overwhelming majority of the population of the globe. And during the past few years it is this majority that has been drawn into the struggle for emancipation with extraordinary rapidity, so that in this respect there cannot be the slightest doubt what the final outcome of the world struggle will be. In this sense, the complete victory of

---

2   Karl Marx and Friedrich Engels, *Selected Correspondence*, Progress Publishers, Moscow, 1975, pp. 220-224.

3   Lenin, *Collected Works*, Progress Publishers, 1972, Moscow, Volume 20, pp. 393-454.

socialism is fully and absolutely assured.[4]

Communist parties rapidly formed in Asia and Africa—in India in 1920 (according to the Communist Party of India (Marxist), in 1925 according to the Communist Party of India), in China and South Africa in 1921, and so on. Communist parties emerged in the Arab world, with the Iraqi party being founded in 1934.

Since Lenin's identification of the fundamental trajectory towards "the complete victory of socialism," nearly all significant subsequent developments in the theory and practice of Marxism have built on and arisen from this fundamental shift. (Be it noted in passing that Gramsci's work, 'Some Aspects of the Southern Question' locates him clearly within this paradigm.)

It is against this historical and theoretical background that we can best appreciate that Dr. Ibrahim Allawi, whose major work is published here in English for the first time, has made a unique and original contribution to Marxist theory.

It should be further noted at this point that many of the greatest contributions to the theory and practice of the revolution have arisen from the bitterness of defeat. It was from the decimation of the Communist Party of China in the 1927 Shanghai Massacre that Mao Zedong could advance probably his single greatest contribution to the application and development of Marxism, outlining how, in a large, semi-colonial, semi-feudal country, as China was at the time, the revolution could be won, and the path to socialism opened up. Mao asserted, and went on to show, that a Marxist-Leninist party could represent and embody working class political leadership, but in accordance with the country's demographics, social system, and class composition—in this case with the peasantry constituting the main force in the revolution. This further entailed basing the revolutionary forces in the countryside, building stable revolutionary base areas, waging a protracted people's war, surrounding the cities from the countryside and ultimately seizing nationwide political power by armed force. This also proved to be the model that was basically applied to the revolution in countries as varied as Vietnam, Laos, Cambodia, Yugoslavia, Albania, Cuba, Mozambique,

---

4   Lenin, *Collected Works*, 2nd English Edition, Progress Publishers, Moscow, 1965, Volume 33, pp. 487 - 502.

Zimbabwe, Eritrea, and Guinea Bissau, among others.

Allawi's contributions come into this same category. Communism came to enjoy huge popularity in Iraq. By the late 1950s its Communist Party was the second strongest party outside of the socialist camp, surpassed only by the Indonesian party. It stood at the head of a movement of millions and the victory of the Iraqi revolution seemed a more than realistic prospect. Some people estimate that up to one in eight of the population joined the party's May Day march in 1958.

However, the Iraqi Communist Party fell victim to Khrushchev's appeasement of US imperialism and the resultant split in the international communist movement.

The split in the international movement inevitably led to splits in the national and Iraq proved to be no exception. After several years of struggle, this culminated in the formation of the Communist Party of Iraq (Central Command) in 1967, with Allawi among the key leaders and later its long-serving Secretary-General. The party enjoyed significant mass support, for example it won the leadership of the mass student union and Allawi himself was elected to the leadership of the powerful Iraqi Engineers Syndicate.

Meanwhile, the other side of the split, which retained the name of Communist Party of Iraq followed the line of the 'non-capitalist road of development' developed by the Soviet Communist Party, which, whatever its actual or potential merits, also dovetailed neatly with the perceived requirements and exigencies of Soviet foreign policy. This led it in time to join the Ba'thist government in a National Progressive Front and then to a bloody dénouement. Later, this party accepted a position for its Secretary-General in the Iraqi Governing Council established by the American occupation.

Allawi and his comrades took a different road—that of armed struggle, inspired by the experience of the Chinese revolution, the Vietnamese people's war of liberation, and the surging tide of national liberation struggles at that time.

This armed struggle, too, went down to bloody defeat amidst terrible repression.

But Allawi did not give way to despondency, join a fashionable trend of reneging, or forget his original aspiration. Rather, in the phrase most often associated with Amilcar Cabral, the Marxist leader of the liberation struggle in Guinea-Bissau, he 'returned to the source'—by embarking on a deep process of study and reflection.

In returning to the source, Allawi drank from two wells—going deeply into Islamic philosophy, history and culture as well as critically assessing the historical experience of actually existing socialism on the basis of the original theories and precepts of Marx, Engels, and Lenin.

The results of his explorations are presented here.

With regard to his explorations in Islam, some might seek to present this as an accommodation to, or adaptation of, an Islamic 'Liberation Theology.' This cannot be entirely dismissed. However (and whilst it clearly and rightly does not in any way preclude freedom of religious belief and worship), Allawi does not engage in theism, or concern himself with the existence or otherwise of a deity or deities, but rather addresses the essentially emancipatory and socialistic message contained within Islamic philosophy, which is expressed in a religious form consistent with the times.

In so doing, he seeks to make the essential message of socialism, the true core of Marxism, comprehensible, reasonable and attractive to the masses of Iraqi people, doubtless including many party members and communist militants. For want of a better term, he seeks to create a 'socialism with Iraqi characteristics.'

More pertinent than any comparison with Liberation Theology is the remarkable way that Allawi's ideas here prefigure Xi Jinping's thesis of the "two integrations," which explores the highly complementary nature and mutually reinforcing synergy of traditional Chinese culture and civilization on the one hand and Marxism on the other.

As the Chinese leader explained in June 2023:

> Given the profound foundations of our venerable 5,000-year-old civilization, the only path for pioneering and developing Chinese socialism is to integrate the basic tenets of Marxism with China's specific realities and the best of its traditional culture ('two integrations'). This systematic conclusion has been derived from our extensive explorations of Chinese socialism. We have always emphasized integrating the basic tenets of Marxism with China's specific realities and have now officially brought forward the integration of the basic

tenets of Marxism with China's fine traditional culture. As I once stated, without the 5,000-year-old Chinese civilization, where would the Chinese characteristics come from?

The 'two integrations' is not a far-fetched proposition. Despite their distinct origins, Marxism and traditional Chinese culture exhibit remarkable congruence. For instance, the social principles of pursuing the common good for all and acting in good faith and being friendly to others resonate harmoniously with the ideals and convictions of communism and socialism; the governing concepts of regarding the people as the foundation of the state and governing by virtue align seamlessly with the political principle of putting the people first; and the practices of discarding the outdated in favor of the new and ceaselessly pursuing self-improvement correspond faithfully to the revolutionary spirit of Communists. Marxism sees the essence of man from the angle of social relations, while in Chinese culture, people are defined by their relationships with their family, their country, and the world. Both reject the notion of viewing humans as isolated entities.[5]

In going back to the classical canon of Marxism in order to understand and explain the historical experience of attempts to build socialism up to time of writing, like many Western Marxists, and indeed like at least the early stages of the 'Cultural Revolution' in China, Allawi takes as his starting point the Paris Commune of 1871.

In many ways, this is entirely reasonable, even essential. Albeit that it extended only to a single city, and endured for a tragically short time, it was the only clear example and reference point of the working class in power that was available for Marx and Engels to study and its emphasis on direct democracy and accountability was undoubtedly attractive to Allawi, faced with the bureaucratic and sclerotic reality of the latter day Soviet Union and a number of its allied countries.

To what extent the prescriptions developed by Allawi for a Mushtarak socialism in Iraq would have proved feasible, faced with the national, regional and global realities that a possible socialist Iraq could have been expected to face, is something we cannot know.

There could be many reasons why some of the precise prescriptions advanced by Lenin in his *State and Revolution* failed to be materialized

---

[5] Jinping, Xi, 'Speech at the Meeting on Cultural Inheritance and Development,' *Qiushi*, 2023, reprinted on Friends of Socialist China, accessible online at https://socialistchina.org/2023/12/30/xi-jinping-integrate-the-basic-tenets-of-marxism-with-chinas-specific-realities-and-the-best-of-its-traditional-culture/

(as Allawi himself hints at with reference to the Stalin period), but one of them is surely the internal and external challenges faced by the Soviet state, which never enjoyed a single day of true peace in the face of the imperialist threat and challenge.

Marx, Engels, and Lenin yielded to no one in their affirmation of the Paris Commune, but as required by the scientific method, they also did not hesitate to criticize its shortcomings. Far from idealizing the 'extreme democracy' of the Commune, Marx observed that, "the Central Committee surrendered its power too soon to make way for the Commune."

In his 1908 article, 'Lessons of the Commune,' Lenin wrote:

> But two mistakes destroyed the fruits of the splendid victory. The proletariat stopped half-way: instead of setting about 'expropriating the expropriators,' it allowed itself to be led astray by dreams of establishing a higher justice in the country united by a common national task; such institutions as the banks, for example, were not taken over, and Proudhonist theories about a 'just exchange,' etc., still prevailed among the socialists. The second mistake was excessive magnanimity on the part of the proletariat: instead of destroying its enemies it sought to exert moral influence on them; it underestimated the significance of direct military operations in civil war, and instead of launching a resolute offensive against Versailles that would have crowned its victory in Paris, it tarried and gave the Versailles government time to gather the dark forces and prepare for the blood-soaked week of May.[6]

And in his 'First Congress of the Communist International: Theses and Report on Bourgeois Democracy and the Dictatorship of the Proletariat,' Lenin states: "The Paris Commune took the first epoch-making step along this path. The Soviet system has taken the second."[7]

Implicit in this is that Soviet power constitutes a more advanced experience than the Paris Commune. The latter is the first word, not the last, in the exercise of power by the working class.

But whatever might be said of Allawi's bold attempt to imagine and outline a more democratic socialist future, and whilst Marxists are not fortune tellers, anyone who had been able to read his work when it was first published in Arabic in 1983, should not have been taken by com-

---

[6] Lenin, *Collected Works*, Progress Publishers, 1972, Moscow, Volume 13, pp. 475-478.

[7] Lenin, *Collected Works*, Progress Publishers, 1972, Moscow, Volume 28, pp. 455-477.

plete surprise when the USSR and the East European socialist countries collapsed in ignominy less than a decade later—when, in Xi Jinping's words, "nobody was man enough to stand up and resist."

It can be unwise or even invidious to attempt to project views of subsequent developments onto those who are no longer with us. However, just as Allawi's study of Marxist theory and the historical experience of Soviet socialism provides important clues to the ultimate failure of the first sustained socialist experiment, so his explorations of the socialist thread in Islamic philosophy—even its clear echo in the *Communist Manifesto*—provides a comparative framework which can help us to understand why it was China, the Democratic People's Republic of Korea, Cuba, Vietnam, and Laos that survived the tidal wave that swept away socialism in other countries. Whatever the challenges faced by these five countries, and whatever their shortcomings, they all experienced a deep and profound—not superficial as was the case in much of Eastern Europe—social revolution, a revolution made by the masses of the people, and not imposed by bureaucratic diktat; and each has gone on to translate Marxism into the respective national language, enriching and developing it through the process of fusion with historical and cultural traditions and national sentiments, the theoretical and practical innovations of their revolutionary leaders, and above all, the social practice, sacrifice, and hopes and dreams of countless millions of people.

Likewise, at time of writing, Allawi could not have been expected to foresee the phenomenal economic rise of China. But what if he could look today at Xi Jinping's concept of 'whole process people's democracy,' where "the running of the country by the people is the essence and heart of socialist democracy. The very purpose of developing socialist democracy is to give full expression to the will of the people, protect their rights and interests, spark their creativity, and provide a system of institutions to ensure that it is they who run the country";[8] along with China's revival of cooperative forms of ownership, not to mention the exciting if challenging new prospects for socialism in Latin America, not least the Commune movement in Venezuela? It does not seem un-

---

8   Jinping, Xi, 'Speech at the Central People's Congress Work Conference,' *Quishi*, 2022, reprinted on Friends of Socialist China, accessible online at https://socialistchina.org/2024/04/24/developing-whole-process-peoples-democracy-and-ensuring-the-people-run-the-country/

reasonable to postulate that he would have seen, and identified with, comrades grappling with the same challenges that he, too, had fearlessly taken up.

Ibrahim Allawi is one of many great Global South Marxists whose work has simply not been known in the Global North in particular, but whose vision and insights, born from the triumphs, vicissitudes, and tragedies of revolutionary praxis, need to be known, debated and studied by those who aspire to a better world. The working-class movement therefore owes an immense debt of gratitude to his comrades for their translation and editing, and to the comrades of Iskra Books for believing in the project and making it possible, along with everything they do.

I'll make two final points.

First, after *Al-Mushtarak*'s broad historical and theoretical sweep, this book ends not with a summation, but by addressing the question of Palestine as central to the liberation of the Arab people as a whole.

Far from being incongruous, this serves to remind us of the words etched on Marx's tomb that, "the philosophers have only *interpreted* the world, in various ways. The point, however, is to *change* it."

This was surely Allawi's purpose in writing and that to which he dedicated his life. Writing now, when the heroic Palestinian people remain defiant, undaunted and undefeated in the face of the tenth month of a Nazi-like war of genocidal aggression by the Zionist state, can one doubt the acuity of his political analysis and foresight here?

Lastly, like many revolutionaries—indeed, like Marx himself—Allawi was all too familiar with the pain of exile. Much of his work on *Al-Mushtarak* was done whilst living in the south London district of East Dulwich. As he dug deep into the lessons of the Paris Commune, it is intriguing to wonder if he was ever aware that, a century before, his East Dulwich exile was shared by one of the most famous Communards, namely Louise Michel, following her release from captivity in Kanaky, the French colony of New Caledonia, whose own unfinished liberation struggle is also making headlines today.

Allawi would surely have been moved by her being one of the few Communards whose stand with the proletariat of Paris was fused with that of colonially oppressed peoples. Together, Michel and Allawi stand as true fighters for the liberation of the proletariat, independent of all nationality, being conscious that, in winning its own emancipation, it is the working class that is destined to liberate all humanity.

In the course of that protracted journey, *Reading in Al-Mushtarak* provides not only an analysis of why the old world must give way to the new, but also a glimpse of what that new world might look like.

FOREWORD II

A Step Towards a Planetary Mushtarak

Brandon Wolfe-Hunnicutt[1]

The great genius of Marx is that he had to be carried out of Europe for his deepest insights to have any real meaning. This aphorism finds powerful new support in the present volume of theoretical writings of Ibrahim Allawi, the Secretary General of the Iraqi Communist Party (Central Command) from 1978-1992. At a time when much of Western Marxism remains seemingly mired in a hopeless solipsism, it can be particularly refreshing to look to non-Western traditions for conceptual insights.[2]

Allawi's will not be a name familiar to many Western readers. It appears only once in Hannah Batatu's magisterial *The Old Social Classes and the Revolutionary Movements of Iraq: A Study of Iraq's Old Landed Classes and of its Communists, Ba'thists and Free Officers*.[3] This is likely because Allawi presided over a deeply embittered, and indeed recently split, party—perhaps at the nadir of its existence to that point.[4]

---

[1] Brandon Wolfe-Hunnicutt teaches US and West Asian History at California State University Stanislaus. He is the author of *The Paranoid Style in American Diplomacy: Oil and Arab Nationalism in Iraq* (Stanford, 2021). Correspondence to BWOLFEHUNNICUTT@CSUSTAN.EDU.

[2] Much of what passes for contemporary Western Marxism is indifferent (when not explicitly hostile) to the interests and concerns of what Fanon described as "The Wretched of the Earth." See, for example, Jonas Elvander and Leigh Phillips, "Degrowth is Not the Answer to Climate Change," *Jacobin*, Jan 8, 2023; Matt Huber, "The Problem with Degrowth," *Jacobin*, July 16, 2023. For a more promising non-Western approach, see Ali Kadri, *The Accumulation of Waste: A Political Economy of Systemic Destruction* (Brill, 2023).

[3] Princeton, 1978.

[4] **Ed. Note:** In 1967, the Iraqi Communist party split into two—one side of the split retained

The Communist Party of Iraq (CPI) was and is one of the oldest and most storied communist parties in history of West Asia (or the "Middle East," as the Europeans used to say). The CPI first began to organize in the 1920s as a Marxist study circle that met, not insignificantly, in Baghdad's Haidarkhanah Mosque.[5] With the onset of the Great Depression in 1929, Iraqi commodity prices collapsed, leading to a sharp decline in Iraqi employment and wages. In response to this latest crises of international capitalism, the Iraqi Communist Party leaders also formed the *Jamiyyat Dudd Al-Istimar* (The Association Against Colonialism) in March 1935.

At the time, Iraq was firmly integrated into the British imperial system, and the party faced severe repression at the hands of the neo-colonial Hashemite Monarchy imposed on the country after the defeat of the Ottoman Empire in WWI. Despite this repression, the CPI organized underground and led a broad national resistance to imperialism and neocolonialism and in defense of Iraqi workers and peasants.

Aligned with the Soviet Union, the CPI fell into a severe crisis in 1948, when the Soviet Union supported the UN proposal to partition Palestine into separate Arab and Jewish states. Once the Soviet Union corrected its stance on Palestine (truth be told, after the damage was done and the Israeli Communist Party had already played a part in securing the arms needed to carry out the *Nakba*, or ethnic cleansing of much of Palestine), the CPI's fortunes recovered and, by the early 1950s, was the country's leading force against Zionism, imperialism, and feudalism. In the late 1950s, it helped to organize a broad National Front that unified all major opposition parties and laid the groundwork for the so-called Free Officers' Revolution that came in July 1958.

That revolution, a major watershed event in the history of West Asia, and with major reverberations throughout the Mediterranean Basin, brought the Iraqi Communist Party to the precipice of state power.

---

the name Iraqi Communist Party, occasionally identified by adding (Central Leadership), and the other faction, headed by Ibrahim Allawi, is referred to as the ICP (Central Command). See Appendix for a timeline of the split.

5   Batatu, *The Old Social Classes*, p. 393. **Ed. Note:** Alongside other Marxist cells in Basra and Nasiriyah, the party was eventually founded in 1934 by Yousif Salman Farhad, "Comrade Fahd," a worker from the country's south.

For a time, the CPI exercised what Batatu refers to as "dual power"—acting as the main force of organized support for General Abd al-Karim Qasim's revolutionary regime.

Under Qasim and the Communists, Iraq withdrew from the US-organized security alliance known as the "Baghdad Pact," opened relations with the Soviet Union, began nationalizing its oil sector, built public housing for displaced peasants, and undertook an impressive national health and literacy campaign. As part of this campaign, Qasim appointed Naziha al-Dulaimi, a Baghdad gynecologist and an important leader of the Communist movement, as Iraq's new minister of municipalities. In so doing, al-Dulaimi became the first woman to hold a cabinet position in West Asia.

Predictably, Qasim's progressivism ran afoul of the United States, which soon dispatched its coup-making goons to the region to overturn Iraq's impressive strides toward a truly just society. That coup, which unfolded in February 1963, first brought the Ba'th Party to power in Iraq and spelled doom for the Communists. Under the watchful eye of the CIA, Iraqi death squads rounded up and executed the party's leadership and much of its rank-and-file support.

The CPI never truly recovered from the devastations of 1963. With the decimation of the party, the mantle of the left largely passed to the *Nasiriyun*—or followers of Egyptian President Gamal Abdel Nasser, who had by this point allied his state with the Soviet Union and set his country, and as much of the region as possible, on the road of Arab Socialism. The remnants of the CPI then worked with the Nasiriyun to overthrow the Ba'th in November 1963, and for a time, Iraq rejoined the struggle to create a just society. The CPI was no longer at the forefront of the movement, but it helped to shift the terrain of political struggle in Iraq in the mid-1960s. So much so, that when the Ba'th launched a new bid for power in 1968, the Ba'th found that it would have to correct the error of its previous way and go into coalition with the CPI.[6]

---

6 **Ed. Note:** It was in this period that the split between the more reformist and revolutionary elements was forming. Ibrahim's Allawi's activities gradually won his section of the party important elections for the students union of Iraq in the period 1963-67 and also the influential Iraqi engineers union, with Allawi elected as president. Allawi and close comrade Khalid Ahmed Zaki formed the 'revolutionary group' inside the communist party which opposed the leadership's revisionist policy, following the USSR's commands, and eventually leading to the split of the party in 1967.

The Ba'th entreaty to the left split the Communist movement, with one faction of the party refusing to join the coalition known as the National Patriotic Front. It is this split that is apparent in Allawi's meditations on questions of state and party in this translated volume. This factional split aside, the National Patriotic Front presided over a new golden age in Iraq in the 1970s. It accelerated health, literacy, and housing programs, and then used the good will among the people that such programs garnered to carry through a historical nationalization of the Iraqi oil industry in 1972-73. By the late 1970s, Iraq had developed one of the most advanced societies in the world.

The fortunes of Iraq, and its Communists in particular, took a turn for the worse in 1978, when Saddam Hussein overthrew his long-time patron General Hasan al-Bakr, and seized the power of the presidency for himself.[7] Once in power, Hussein unleashed a severe crackdown on the CPI, and allied his regime with the United States against the revolutionary government of Iran that took shape in 1979.

After receiving a "green light" from the Carter administration, Hussein invaded Iran in September 1980, thereby initiating the long bloody struggle that persisted until 1988. It was in this period of Iraq's deviation from the path of Third World solidarity that Allawi assumed leadership of the Central Command faction of the Iraqi Communist Party. It is this anguish about the state and its army that comes through in Allawi's translated text.

Allawi's translated text gives us an important opportunity to think through appropriate organizational forms for a popular liberation. He was, of course, thinking through all of this from a truly disadvantaged position. And so, some of his meditations on the state and its army reflect that historically specific subject position. But perhaps more significant and enduring than his anguish over the state to which Iraq had fallen (again, he was writing at the very moment that Hussein was formalizing his alliance with Donald Rumsfeld and the US), are his efforts to synthesize Marxist theory with Islamic political philosophy.

---

7   Ed. Note: The Ba'thist government persecuted Allawi's Central Command faction as early as 1968 with hundreds executed. The right-wing Central Committee leadership went into coalition with the Ba'th regime. However, this was also subsequently attacked by Saddam later after it had outgrown its usefulness.

Quite often, communist parties in the Third World faltered on the difficulty that they faced in importing historically specific European political categories into their own societies. Marx may have articulated universal insights, but many of those who came after interpreted those insights in their own particular (and sometimes sectarian) ways. The more successful move, as we see with figures such as the Iranian revolutionary theorist Dr. Ali Shariati, was to translate the (universal) spirit rather than the (particular) letter.[8]

Marx was tapping into a universal spirit from a particular European geography. But access to that universal spirit, what the philosopher Ernst Bloch described as the "Aristotelian Left," was only accessible to Marx and his fellow Europeans because of the theoretical elaborations afforded by the Islamicate.[9] As Allawi shows, it was the contributions of Medieval scientists and philosophers such as Al-Razi, Al-Farabi, Ibn Sina, Al-Biruni, Ibn Khaldun, and Ibn Rushd that made it possible for intellectual descendants such as Marx to envision a Virtuous City, or Mushtarak, as Allawi puts it.

This question of translating concepts of the Virtuous City is worth pondering. In this connection, it is worth recalling that Al-Kindi Circle (Al-Farbi's precursor), began with literal translations of what they thought was Aristotle. But it took another few generations of work for Arab philosophers to translate literal Greek manuscripts into the organic poetry of the Arabic language. Once the spirit, rather than just the letter, was translated into Arabic, it became clear that works attributed to Aristotle (a "historical materialist," as we would say) were in fact created by Plotinus (a neo-Platonic "idealist," as we would say). And then it took several more generations of philosophical work for Ibn Sina and others to realize that Aristotle himself had misperceived, or at least miscommunicated, the universal spirit in certain ways. Ibn Sina then took it upon himself to correct the errors in Aristotle and put forward an entirely new system free of the logical gaps found in Aristotle, or the

---

8   See Evrand Abrahamian, "Ali Shari'ati: Ideologue for the Iranian Revolution," *MERIP* no. 102 (1982).

9   Ernst Bloch, *Avicenna and the Aristotelian Left*, trans. Loren Goldman and Peter Thompson (Columbia University Press, 2019). For a useful introduction to the history of philosophy in the Islamic world, see Peter Adamson, *History of Philosophy Without Any Gaps* (King's College London, 2013), podcast episodes 120-45, https://historyofphilosophy.net/avicenna-life-works.

First Teacher as he was known. It was this corrected and clarified Aristotelianism that medieval Christian scribes found in Toledo, Palermo, and Antioch, that was then handed down to Marx. (Ibn Sina may have rejected Aristotle's system in favor of his own, but his clarifications of Aristotle nonetheless formed the basis for Europe's eventual incorporation of Aristotelian thought.)

It is with this attention to the nuances of translation that readers should approach Allows text. Allawi's effort to root the doctrines of Communism within the traditions Islamic political philosophy offers great promise to those of us in the west groping our way toward a conceptual lens through which we might make sense of the world in which we find ourselves. In so doing, we in the west might do well to remember that "we were never modern," and that to be in true solidarity with those on the front lines fighting for a better world, some of us must shed our sectarian prejudices against something called "religion."[10] Secularism is its own fetishized religion, and for whatever it is or was worth, it is imperative that we remember that secularism abandoned the people most in need of liberation a long time ago. It is therefore fitting that Iraqi Communism was first organized in the space provided by Baghdad's Haidarkhanah Mosque.

Rooting ourselves in Islamic political philosophy, we can then take to heart the more practical steps that Allawi sets out for us. We see the future lies in a liberated Palestine, that pan-Arab unity is a necessary step toward a truly planetary Mushtarak (as is the case with pan-Islamic, pan-African, pan-American, and pan-Asian unities). And we can see that a reconstituted and expanded New Silk Road is how we get there.

---

10   Abdal Jawad Omar, "The Question of Hamas and the Left," *Mondoweiss*, May 24, 2024.

EDITOR'S INTRODUCTION

ALI AL-ASSAM & MAJED ALLAWI

READING in *Al-Mushtarak* is our translation and minor editing of the document *Al-Mushtarak*, originally issued in 1983 in Iraq as a programmatic document addressing the new tasks of the Iraqi revolution during that period. It was prepared by the Central Command of the Iraqi Communist Party based on a review of experiences from modern socialist revolutions, as well as an examination of Islamic societies and the emerging conditions in Iraq.

Al-Mushtarak represents a significant development in socialist thought, drawing on the experiences of the Iraqi and global communist movement. It was primarily authored by the late Dr. Ibrahim Allawi, the Secretary-General of the Iraqi Communist Party (Central Command) during the 1970s, 1980s, and 1990s.

The document establishes the foundations for a path towards creating advanced democratic societies that are free from the exploitation of humans or nations. It also discusses the basis of collaborative thought in Islamic history and emphasizes the positive role that Islamic collaborative philosophical heritage can play in effecting positive change in Iraq. As stated in *Al-Mushtarak*:

> Islam has embraced the principle of collaboration among Muslims and has considered land, minerals, and water as the property of God, thus the collective property of the entire Islamic community. It is impermissible for anyone to monopolize them or act against the public interests of the entire nation. This principle formed the basis of the *Kharaj* system, the agricultural system in Islam. The *Communist Manifesto* of 1848 referred to this advanced economic system for the first time, listing it as the primary demand among several others in its second section: '1. Abolition of Private Ownership of Land and Making All Land Revenues Public.'

We firmly believe that the significance of *Al-Mushtarak* goes beyond simply delineating the path towards democratic socialism and establishing a framework for people's democracy and a sharing economy following the overthrow of dictatorial regimes. It also emphasizes the crucial role of establishing cooperative institutions as an integral part of the pursuit of political transformation. This is demonstrated by successful instances like the Mondragon cooperatives in Spain, and the cooperatives and social enterprises in the People's Republic of China, these models effectively exemplify the importance of fostering cooperative initiatives within this approach.

Finally, it is important to note that specific details related to the Iraqi political scene at the time have been excluded, as they are not crucial to the main sections covering the program for democratic socialism and Islamic history. These sections remain unchanged.

We welcome any language corrections, thoughts, or comments you may have regarding *Al-Mushtarak*, and you can email them to MUSHTAREK@MUSHTAREK.ORG.

Why Al-Mushtarak?
UPDATING THE ORIGINAL 1983 TEXT TO REFLECT THE CONTEMPORARY POLITICAL SITUATION AS OF 2024

Al-Mushtarak was written in 1983, amidst the Iran-Iraq War, following a series of military setbacks experienced by Saddam Hussein's regime. During this period, a prevailing sense of optimism pervaded among various segments and nationalities of the Iraqi population, as they eagerly anticipated the impending collapse of the Ba'th regime and the cessation of the darkness that had engulfed Iraq. Their hopes extended towards an end to the bloodshed, forced displacement, and the erosion of human dignity. However, it took another two decades for the regime to eventually fall, which came about in 2003 as a result of the American invasion of Iraq. Unfortunately, the fall of the regime did not alleviate the suffering of the Iraqi people but rather it manifested in new forms of hardship.

In spite of the Iraqi people's hopeful anticipation for the downfall of Saddam Hussein's regime, the occupying American forces sought to enforce a new form of colonial occupation through military might and destructive means. This entailed dismantling the various components of the Iraqi state, assuming control over oil resources, and implementing the Biden project, which aimed to arbitrarily divide Iraq along ethnic lines, thereby ensuring U.S. domination over a weakened country. While the Iraqi people managed to establish popular elections despite resistance from the occupiers, the political process has been operating within a framework rooted in colonial design. This framework is characterized by a constitution that is unchangeable in certain aspects (as outlined in Article 142), ultimately leading to the institutionalization of political sectarianism, corruption, the division of Iraq, and the consolidation of control over its resources.

Iraq emerged from the grip of a repressive regime, initially fostered by colonial influences, only to descend into another period of darkness. This darkness witnessed the rise of brutal and extremist groups like Daesh (ISIS), who managed to exert control over vast regions of our country. However, thanks to the heroic sacrifices of the Popular Mobilization Forces and the armed forces, these forces were ultimately defeated. Nevertheless, the political crisis persisted, with a corrupt political system that emerged as a consequence of the Bremer political composition. This system only brought backwardness and misery to the Iraqi people, exacerbating their hardships.

The issue of a political alternative, which the majority of the Iraqi people agree on, has become an urgent task that does not accept postponement or procrastination: What political system will ensure our people's exit from the eras of darkness, terrorism, wars, destruction, and corruption? What political institutions will guarantee the people's democratic freedoms and restore human dignity in Iraq? Which political forces are nominated to lead the people's struggle towards national liberation, democracy, and social progress? And what is the way out of the current crisis facing the country?

There is no doubt that one of the most important intellectual problems that need to be solved is determining the correct relationship between the democratic and socialist revolutions. Iraqi society today faces not the task of the socialist revolution but the national democratic revolution. However, this revolution cannot be led by the prevailing political forces, whose institutions are steeped in corruption and operate within the current constitutional fabric, but requires new political institutions and forces representing millions of Iraqi workers in all their categories, institutions that follow the path of economic-political independence and self-reliance, benefiting from the rich experiences of leftist movements, cooperatives, and trade union movements in the world over the past fifty years.

The concept of *Al-Mushtarak* [the commons] embodies the essence of modern socialist revolutions, drawing inspiration from Arab-Islamic history and the traditions of the Iraqi people. It serves as a powerful tool for constructing contemporary, economically prosperous self-sustaining institutions, even in the face of a corrupt state. These democratic institutions, forming a cooperative ecosystem, will unite the Iraqi people in their pursuit of progress, a free homeland, and a blissful populace. Together, they will forge a path towards a brighter future filled with hope and shared prosperity, leveraging the transformative potential of the modern communications revolution.

The upcoming chapters are our translation of the original 1983 study of *Al-Mushtarak* with very minor, noted, changes.

On Terminology

The ancients were precise in expressing social and philosophical concepts and therefore developed precise terminology that disappeared with their societies and remained distant from everyday use. Some translators and modern writers have resorted to using foreign words without making a serious attempt to find their counterparts in the Arabic language. This linguistic approach can serve the limited purpose of quickly translating political and social texts, but it quickly becomes a source of confusion and misunderstanding when there is a need to compare these concepts to old concepts in order to better understand the characteristics of our society and its historical formation. Let us take the terms 'socialism' and 'communism' as an example.

It is known that these words entered the Arabic language, where modern socialist movements emerged, through translations of their counterparts in European languages. When Arab writers, such as Jamal al-Din al-Afghani and Muhammad Abduh, took up these concepts, they initially used the closest equivalent, who used the term *ijtima'iyah* [social] as an equivalent to the French and English word 'socialism,' and the term *shiyou yah* [communism] as a translation of the European word 'communism.'[1] Then new terms appeared in the writings of intellectuals influenced by European thought, such as Salama Musa, who used the word *ishtiraki yah* [socialist] in his books *Superman* and *Socialism*, which were published in 1910 and 1913, respectively. There is a big difference between the concepts of the *ijtima'iyah* [social] and *ishtiraki yah* [socialism] even though both terms were used as equivalents to the European word 'socialism.' As for the term *shiyou iyah* as an equivalent to 'communism,' it appears to have become an accepted translation by all writers, as seen in Salama Musa's aforementioned book, where he spoke in 1910 of "...the socialist tendency which ended in communism [*shiyou iyah*] in the farthest regions of Europe," to distinguish between the two concepts.

When we compare these translations of European concepts with their linguistic origins, we find clear differences from their counterparts in the Arabic language, especially regarding the word 'socialism' commonly used today to refer to the social system advocated by Marxism as a first historical stage towards communism. The word 'socialism' translated in Arabic as *al-istirākīyah* is derived from the word 'social' which as some European dictionaries mention is derived from the Latin word *socius* meaning 'companion, ally, or clan.' The word 'social' has other meanings that it acquires from its context in speech, for example, concepts related to social life, such as 'social relations' in English and *rapports sociaux* in French, which are different from the concept of socialism as a political movement or a certain social pattern.[2]

We can understand the reason from what has been presented for the multiplicity of Arabic equivalents for the word 'socialism' when translated. When Muhammad Abduh translated it as *al-ijtimā'īyah*, it was an accurate translation in terms of grammatical meaning, while translat-

[1] See Jamal al-Din al-Afghani's letter 'In response to the materialists,' Hyderabad 1879, Dar al-Hilal edition, Cairo, 1973, p.17.

[2] The concept of *'socialisme'* in French was derived from the English word 'socialism' since 1822, or the Italian word *'socialismo'* since 1803, as noted by the French linguist Robert, the author of the famous French dictionary bearing his name. Therefore, the appearance of this word in European languages has undergone a historical development rather than a simple linguistic derivation.

ing it as *al-istirākīyah* was not linguistically accurate, as 'social' does not necessarily mean the participation in ownership of properties and means of production. However, the use of the term 'socialism' at the time also indicated a political need that required it to be distinguished as a revolutionary movement that aimed to serve the interests of the labor force. On the other hand, the word *al-ijtimā'īyah* in Arabic, despite its linguistic accuracy, does not provide the necessary feature that supporters of socialism such as Salama Moussa and then Arab Marxists aimed for.

Therefore, the problem has exceeded linguistic boundaries into political concepts, reflecting fundamental social differences between European and Islamic-Arabic circumstances. European middle-class societies and capitalism are based on the concept of individual private ownership of means of production and land. Therefore, calls for social ownership became revolutionary in relation to the dominant concept of individual ownership at the time. Hence, progressive movements called themselves "socialist." In countries that were ruled by Islamic law for long periods, the situation is different, where the state owns land, rivers, and major means of production. Private ownership, alongside state ownership, mainly belonged to senior officials and depended, therefore, to a large extent on their positions in the state apparatus. Such a situation, as we will see, made the call for 'social' ownership in Islam a meaningless demand and a call for an existing reality. Therefore, the concept of 'social' loses its revolutionary meaning as a movement that expresses the interests of the working class. Hence, the translation of Jamal al-Din al-Afghani and Muhammad Abdu's use of the term 'social' did not gain acceptance among the leftist movement in Arab countries, and the use of 'socialism' became widespread, despite its clear difference from its European origins. In fact, the Arabic word *al-ishtirākīyah* corresponds to the European word 'communism' because both are derived from the concept of sharing. However, the use of the term 'communism' has made this linguistic difference between the term and the concept acceptable and widely recognized due to its long use.

Another problem arises when translating the French word *commune*, where Marxist translators into Arabic have traditionally translated it as *musha'a* [common] or kept the words 'commune' and 'communard' as they are. However, accepting this terminological usage creates many obstacles in understanding ancient Islamic texts, which constitute a fundamental heritage for any correct understanding of the social and political development of Islamic societies, including Iraq.

Therefore, we have decided to use the ancient Arabic word with deep connotations, *Al-Mushtarak* [the commons], as a counterpart to the concept of the 'commune' in Marxist literature. This is a valid choice, as Marx and Engels used old German terms, as Lenin pointed out, to translate the word 'commune.' Lenin also noted that the Russian language lacks a word that corresponds to the meaning of this term, so he suggested using the same French word to refer to 'commune.'

The reason we chose to use the word *Al-Mushtarak* is the numerous pre-Islamic and Islamic Arabic texts indicating that this term is almost synonymous with the word 'communal,' with a fundamental difference being that participation presupposes shared individuals and people, while communal means things that are shared. It is stated in a Hadith:

> The partner is better than the companion, and the companion is better than the neighbor.[3]

The author of the dictionary interpreted this Hadith as follows:

> He meant by the partner the one who participates in the communal sharing.

The linguistic difference between participation and communal sharing becomes clear, and this confirms that the word *Al-Mushtarak* presupposes a human group as a fundamental basis before shared things and properties. To highlight the role of human beings in this concept, it is of special importance in the social system. We hope that this will become clear in the following chapters. This issue was of interest to Marx and Engels, as they explained the difference between the terms 'socialism' and 'communism' (in the common meaning of the terms). Engels wrote in the introduction to the *Communist Manifesto* in 1890:

> ...in 1847, socialism was a middle-class movement, communism a working-class movement.[4]

The term 'social-democrat,' which is usually translated in Arabic as 'democracy-socialism' or sometimes with the first word preceding the

---

3   See Jamal al-Din al-Afghani's letter 'In response to the materialists,' Hyderabad 1879, Dar al-Hilal edition, Cairo, 1973, p.17.

4   *Preface to the 1888 English edition* as available from marxists.org.

second, has been proposed by Engels to be replaced with the word 'communist' to match the goals of the Marxist movement and its scientific concepts.[5] For the same reason, Lenin proposed in 1917 to change the name of the Russian Social Democratic Labour Party to the All-Russian Communist Party and explained the important political purpose of this change in his April Theses.[6]

To avoid confusion between these terms and the concept of democracy under socialism, we have used the translation 'social democracy' for the movements and parties, according to the European linguistic meaning of this term. Where the term 'socialist democracy' appears on the following pages, it does not refer to the Second International parties and the Kautsky school, but to proletarian democracy under socialism. It is known that 'social democracy' is a derived term from European linguistic roots used to distinguish this movement from 'political democracy,' which was primarily associated with bourgeois liberal parties in Europe. The term 'social democracy' spread in the second half of the last century as a distinctive symbol for socialist and labor parties seeking to benefit from legal working conditions and participate in parliamentary battles. This term no longer represents the Marxist movement, especially after the socialist October Revolution, where most of the Second International parties turned into organizations that served liberal bourgeois interests, despite their historical roots and membership consisting of workers.

In light of these changes, the Bolshevik Party changed its name to the Communist Party as mentioned earlier, while Marx and Engels replaced every instance of the word 'state' in the program of the German Social Democratic Party for the years 1870 with the word 'commune' meaning *Mushtarak*.

It remains to clarify some other points that are repeated in the following chapters, causing confusion, such as the concept of Islam. When we speak of 'Islam,' we do not mean just the Islamic Sharia defined by the jurists through the Quran and Sunnah and what each school of thought presents of Islamic teachings. Rather, we mean by 'Islam,' wherever it is

---

5   See Lenin, *Selected Works*, Vol. 2, Section 1, Foreign Languages Publishing House, Moscow, 1952, p. 458.

6   Ibid., p.48.

mentioned and as is clear from the context, that period of Iraq's history and the countries that were subjected to Islamic rule for long periods of time, and their social formations adapted to the specific patterns associated with Islamic rule. This definition may be incomplete or imprecise from a scientific perspective, and it may be argued that it can be replaced with commonly used terms such as the Middle Ages or the Byzantine period, etc. However, the lack of applicability of terminologies derived from European history to the situation of Islam, such as the expressions 'medieval' and 'feudal' along with the absence of agreed-upon scientific terminologies about Islamic history, may justify the definition we presented for the concept of 'Islam.'

It is needless to say that the Marxist-Leninist stance towards religion is clear and does not need to be repeated in this document. The intention here is not to reconcile conflicting intellectual trends, but rather to objectively study historical phenomena as much as possible, shedding light on the current situation in our country and exploring the path to the future.

Image 1.2. *Dr. Ibrahim Allawi.*

Image 1.3. Art by Dia Al-Azzawi. *Bilad al-Sawad*, 1994-5.

AL-MUSHTARAK

AL-MUSHTARAK IN ISLAM[1]

The state, in Marxist analyses, is a "machine for the suppression of the oppressed, exploited class."[2] It is a general authority that stands above society to subjugate those who are governed and maintain the conditions of class exploitation and preserve the privileges of the owning class of the means of production. "The state is a manifestation of the fact that society has entered contradiction with itself that cannot be resolved and has become divided into irreconcilable opposites... thus, it requires a force that stands visibly above society, a force that softens the impact and keeps it within the bounds of the 'system.' This force, which emerges from society and which puts itself above it and becomes increasingly separate from it, is the state."[3]

Therefore, the state is a class-repressive machine that appears with the emergence of social classes in society and evolves with the development of classes. The deeper the exploitation and development of productive forces, the more privileges the owners of the means of production enjoy, and in turn, the greater the need to restrain the producers and maintain the conditions of production as it is. As much as the owning class enriches itself from the toil of workers, farmers, and slaves, it finds itself increasingly compelled to resort to violence and to strengthen the state machine against resistance from producers. Thus, the history of civilization reveals two contradictory trends. The progress of technology, production, and science witnessed by the ages of civilization, reinforced the machinery of repression and war, and thereby expanded the powers enjoyed by the state over the governed, on one hand. On the other hand, there was an increasing contraction of real freedoms in human

---

1   **Ed. Note:** Translated here from the original text in the Mushtarak document *Al-Mushtarak in Islam*.

2   Engels, *The Origin of the Family, Private Property and the State*, International Publishers, Moscow, 1942, p. 232.

3   Ibid., p. 225.

societies. Therefore, the development of civilization in class societies is reflected in a general reduction of human freedom.[4] Primitive societies that have not yet known the state are those in which humans organize their lives without the need for a specific repressive machine whose purpose is to suppress opponents.

In this regard, we see that studying stateless primitive societies holds particular importance for understanding the reality of the state and realizing how a human society can function without organized social oppression. This does not mean, of course, that primitive societies did not experience violence and wars, but it means that violence was either an individual matter in which individuals settled issues of revenge and personal disputes, or a phenomenon that expressed the disintegration of those societies and their inability to keep up with production development or their need for food and pasture. Nevertheless, those societies represent, for the study of advanced societies, what embryology represents for the study of biology, that is, discovering "what is most modern in what is most ancient," in Marx's expression.[5] Pre-Islamic era *Al-Jahiliyah* [state of ignorance] societies provide us with a rich field for studying the processes of the emergence of the state among the Arabs and then its development in the era of Islam.

Al-Mushtarak in the Era of Ignorance [Al-Jahiliyah, the Pre-Islamic Era of Arabia]

The history and development of Islam throughout the ages is still far from being scientifically studied, despite the extensive studies and research presented by orientalists. In fact, most of these orientalist studies may have been the cause of delaying the emergence of a scientific con-

---

4　**Ed. Note:** Here the author is comparing class societies with "primitive" non-class, non-state society.

5　**Ed. Note:** We weren't able to find a source for this quote, which the original author included. However, this concept aligns with Marx's broader ideas about historical materialism and the development of social and economic structures. Marx often explored how historical processes and ancient social formations have influenced and shaped modern capitalist societies. Marx's analysis, particularly in works like *Grundrisse* and *A Contribution to the Critique of Political Economy*, and his late in life ethnological studies explore the continuity and transformation of social relations over time.

cept of Islamic history. The study of the pre-Islamic society is even more difficult. Nevertheless, what remains of its poetry and legends, preserved by ancient linguists, provides abundant material for understanding the features of the pre-Islamic era and the nature of the social organizations that existed before Islam.

The term *Jahiliyyah* [ignorance] was used by the Quran to describe the Arab society before Islam. Although it is used here in the context of the usual stance taken by any new movement against a previous or outdated situation, the term has some justification if we consider certain traits known in that primitive society. These include widespread illiteracy, tribal wars, idolatry, gender-based infanticide, and similar practices. However, the pre-Islamic society also had aspects beyond this narrow scope that are worth studying concerning the purposes of this document. It can also be noted that the society in which Islam emerged was less advanced than an earlier stage mentioned in the Quran as the "first *Jahiliyyah*," associated with luxury and display. This reference likely pertains to civilized societies in Yemen, Thamud, and the city-states of trade like the Nabataeans, Hatra, and other cities in Tihama (in the period 12th century BCE to the 6th century CE). In any case, the latter *Jahiliyyah* represents a society in crisis, on the brink of collapse, making a revolution against it a historical necessity realized in the emergence of Islam.

The pre-Islamic society was a tribal society, where the tribe formed the basic social unit, which was a kinship-based association. Within this social unit, basic properties such as camels, sheep, pastures, wells, and water sources remained communal property for long periods. The ethics of *Jahiliyyah* were based on communalism, which involved belonging to a larger group beyond the family, which was the tribe, and sometimes gangs of thieves. The inclination towards communal ownership was evident in their boasts. For example, Urwah bin Alward said:

> I am a man whose pot (food) is shared...

Another poet from the *Jahiliyyah* period said:

> If you ask the kinfolks about me, I am one who is with communal property, you can ask and be sure.

The pasture, water, and fire were shared among people, and naturally, this sharing was based on primitive conditions and barbaric relationships between tribes. The *Jahiliyah* communalism generally did not extend beyond the limits of the tribe, and other tribes were considered enemies whom it was permissible to raid and loot their possessions. Nevertheless, stories link the wars of that society with the beginning of private ownership of land, i.e., the *Himma*. The *Himma* clashed with the traditions of the *Jahiliyah* communalism and was not acceptable according to custom. The first Islam abolished it, but it re-emerged in the era of the Caliphate of Uthman (the third Caliph after Mohammad) and was one of the reasons for the revolution against him.

However, the pre-Islamic cities in which Islam later emerged still carried some remnants of the communal system, but it was a certain level of urbanization and development that differed from the communalism of the Bedouins, although it was still far from the formation of a state. Despite the emergence of some organizations in the cities of Mecca, Yathrib, and Taif, they did not turn into a armed entity separated from the population, and these cities, except for Taif, did not have city walls but were open cities managed by a council of tribal chiefs and nobles who enjoyed great moral authority known as *al-Su'ded*. They did not have their own police or armies, and all residents, except for poor slaves, were armed. The individual's attachment to his weapon was a sign of personal honor, and some *Jahiliyah* people even pawned their bows in exchange for their lives. Mecca was the most developed of these cities, governed by a civil council called *al-Mala* consisting of the city's elders and nobles, who held their meetings in a large house where they decided on the most important issues related to the city. It was called Dar al-Nadwa, and from there, trade caravans were launched, alliances, reconciliations, and war expeditions were held.[6] Mecca was divided into self-governing neighborhoods built in the valleys of the city's mountains and plains around the courtyard of the Kaaba, and each valley or neighborhood includes a branch of the Quraysh tribe headed by one of the nobles or 'lords.' Membership in the council was not only based on rich-

---

6   **Ed. Note:** The Dar al-Nadwah was a council house or assembly hall used by the Quraysh for important discussions and decision-making. It served as the political hub where the heads of the various Quraysh clans would gather to deliberate on matters of common interest, including trade, alliances, and conflicts. The council played a central role in the governance and administration of Mecca.

ness, but also on age and sometimes on personal qualifications. Some sources recall that Quraysh has high ranked Abu Jahl (the fierce opponent of Mohammed in Mecca, who was killed In Bedr, the first battle in Islam) and admitted him to Dar al-Nadwa while he was a youngster.

The sources do not mention the existence of a police force, professional army, or prisons in Mecca and Yathrib before Islam. It appears that Mecca relied on the *Ilaaf* [alliances] which Quraysh had established with other tribes to secure the safety of its caravans. However, in the wars that erupted from time to time, Quraysh seemed to use a kind of 'militia' consisting of the poor Arabs and their mixed-race descendants and groups referred to as "outlaws" by the sources. Some tribal factions had allied with Quraysh to help them in times of danger and were called al-Ahabish, residing outside and close to Mecca. Sources differ on the origin of this tribal formation, but its name is mentioned in history and biography books as having participated in wars under the command of Quraysh and may have later become part of the Meccan 'militia.' What these narratives suggest is that Quraysh did not have a professional military force within Mecca or separate from its inhabitants.

The prevailing economic model in Mecca was based on trade and investment in the pilgrimage seasons, in addition to some handicraft industries that utilized slaves and to a certain extent, the lowly paid workers called *al-Usafāʾ*. Mecca was like a single trading company in which almost all the city's residents participated, making them 'all mixed traders,' as Al-Jahidh said. The word 'mixed' in Arabic means a partner in ownership rights. From this, it is clear that Mecca's *Mushtarak* [commonality] was different from that of the Bedouins and nomadic tribes, as it was based on participating in foreign trade.

The main power was the customs and traditions that previous generations had followed. Therefore, Islam faced resistance from the people of Mecca because of the values it brought that contradicted the prevailing customs in the city. The concept of partnership was, for the *Jahiliyyah* society, an extension of fraternal relationships. The term *Akhwān al-Ṣafāʾ* [the Brethren of Purity] was frequently mentioned in the poetry of the pre-Islamic era, and the movement of the Brethren of Purity, which appeared in the early Abbasid period in Basra and then in Baghdad in the fourth century AH,[7] took its name from it.

Much of the early vitality of Islam was derived from the vitality of the pre-Islamic Jahili communal, Mushtarak system, which, nevertheless, remained limited to the framework of the individual tribe. It is known that such primitive communal social organizations did not have the ability to resist the new economic forces that emerged with the growth of world trade, which led to the transformation of large sectors of Arabian Peninsula societies from pastoral economies to economies based on trade and caravan transportation between major commercial centers. With the growth of global trade, whose main routes passed through the Arabian Peninsula on the eve of the emergence of Islam, the tribal system began to disintegrate, along with the pre-Islamic communal system, paving the way for the emergence of new conditions that evolved after the emergence of Islam.

2. Al-Mushtarak in Islam

The emergence of Islam cannot be understood without recognizing the unique geographic location of the Arabian Peninsula as a meeting point for civilizations and a hub for trade routes between major centers of civilization on earth. Since the closure of trade caravans through Persia and Iraq due to the wars between the Sassanians and Romans, much of this trade shifted to the Arabian Peninsula through Yemen and the Red Sea. Then the Ethiopian occupation of Yemen created a new obstacle in the global trade route to Rome through the cities of Hijaz.[8] This commercial shift led to the transformation of the pastoral economy into a transport and commercial mediation economy, making camels a source of great wealth and transforming some caravan stops into prosperous commercial cities.

This connection to global trade and civilization explains the global

---

7   **Ed. Note:** AH refers to the Arabic or Hijri calendar, dated from Muhammad's journey from Mecca to Medina. For a table of comparative dates, see Appendix I.

8   **Ed. Note:** The Hijaz region is located in the western part of contemporary Saudi Arabia. It extends along the Red Sea coast and includes key cities such as Mecca and Medina, which are of significant religious importance in Islam.

ambitions of Islam, despite its emergence in a small city[9] and an environment influenced by Bedouin culture to some extent. The emergence of Islam and its rapid spread among the Arabs indicated a decline in tribal affiliation in favor of wider human connectivity beyond the tribal framework that led to constant wars and the hindrance of trade routes, and then to the greed of the powerful states surrounding the Arabian Peninsula to control it. Nevertheless, tribal nationalism did not disappear after Islam and remained a social force that influenced the subsequent development of Islam.

The strength of tribalism and strong attachment to idols were factors that led Islam to the concept of absolute monotheism. Islam did not accept the Christian Trinity nor the idea of the 'chosen people,' as European philosophers like Hegel pointed out. This perspective adopted by Islam had serious consequences in the formation of the Islamic state, especially as it continued to maintain some of the pre-Islamic customs and traditions. This paved the way for the integration of means of production with state power, while the democratic aspects of tribal society decreased during the reign of the third Caliph and subsequent Islamic eras.

However, Islam remained influenced by some characteristics of pre-Islamic tribal society, and early Islam in Mecca served as a model for a movement that relied on the poor and weak, while opposing the affluent and wealthy. The Meccan verses of the Quran reflected this in about 36 places, in addition to what was mentioned in the 'Hadith' verses revealed later.

Islam has adopted the principle of sharing among Muslims, and considered the land, minerals, and water as the property of God, meaning the shared property of the entire Islamic nation. It is not permissible for anyone to monopolize or dispose of them in a way that contradicts the public interests of the entire nation. This is why Omar ibn al-Khattab said after the conquest of Iraq: "We have the necks [ownership] of the land."[10]

This ruling was the basis of the *Kharaj* system on which agricul-

---

9   **Ed. Note:** Modern-day Mecca.

10   Al-Amwal: p. 354.

ture was based in Islam. It is important to note here that the *Kharaj* system was an advanced economic system, and it was first mentioned in the modern era in the *Communist Manifesto* of 1848, which included it as the first demand among several other demands in its second section, stating: '1. Abolition of property in land and application of all rents of land to public purposes.'

This demand was emphasized by Engels in 1872 in his work *The Housing Question*, where he stated regarding the tasks of the first stage of communism (socialism): "Abolition of private property in land does not mean the abolition of ground rent, but the transformation of ground rent, through a modified form, into the society."[11]

The *Kharaj* system referred to the notion that agricultural land in occupied countries was public property for all Muslims, and the state leased it to farmers for a specific rent, payable in kind, cash, or both, depending on the circumstances. The *Kharaj* was considered a commonwealth in which the entire community participated, and the Caliph had no right to transfer ownership of *Kharaj* land, seize it, or sell it. It is known that this system was relatively long-standing until the Caliphs began manipulating and withholding *Kharaj* land for officials. However, this principle of social organization based on cooperation continued, as Ibn Sallam, one of the early prominent historians of Islamic economics, said, "The doctrine of Umar ibn al-Khattab was the shared ownership of the Returns..."[12]

Marx also recognized the importance of the Islamic *kharaj* system, writing in a letter dated June 14, 1853, "Muslims were the first to introduce the principle of no private ownership of land in all of Asia."[13]

Sources show that these Arab communal traditions were in contrast to prevailing customs in occupied countries that had ancient class-based civilizations. For example, Al-Jahidh wrote, "The Persians criticized the Arabs for going to war sharing equally, as it is the same as having sharing in war, in wives, and authority."[14]

---

11 Lenin, *Notebooks*: Marxism and the State, Foreign Languages Publishing House, 1935, p. 41.

12 Al-Amwal: 284.

13 Marx and Engels, *Selected Letters*, Progress Publishers, Moscow, 1982, p. 80.

14 Rasa'il al-Jahidh: 33.

We should emphasize here that the Mushtarak that Islam adopted initially was limited to the Islamic community alone, excluding all others. They were the fighters who conquered lands, took control of cities and established their new state. Embracing Islam was a prerequisite for inclusion in this Mushtarak, while non-Muslims were required to pay *jizya* (a tax). Islamic Mushtarak was based on military superiority, or what historians and Islamic jurists called "the communitarianism of the military,"[15] which is fundamentally different from pre-Islamic Mushtarak, which was based on communal ownership of pastures, wells, firewood, etc.

However, the importance of Islamic Mushtarak is not limited to military affairs; it was also applied in planning new cities such as Kufa, Basra [of Iraq], Fustat [part of old Cairo], and Qairouan [in Tunisia]. The planning of these cities shows that they were organized according to a self-governing administrative system for each district or clan, which was then connected, by its leaders, to the center of the city, representing the state. The political organization was based on a system that connects the central authority to the independence of the sectors affiliated with the region. In each sector, its inhabitants were left to organize their private lives according to their tribal ties, yet the conceptual plan for all of these sectors was similar and based on the new traditions that emerged with Islam, without severing their roots from the distant organization of the pre-Islamic Hijazi cities. As we have shown, Mecca was divided into quarters and sub-tribes, each belonging to a specific Quraish clan, then those sub-tribes were connected by Dar al-Nadwa, which was composed of the heads of the Quraish clans.

In the new territories, tribal organization remained the basis for dividing regions, with differences dictated by the particular circumstances of each region. Basra was organized according to *akhmas* [the division into fifth parts], and it remained on this division without significant change until the Abbasid era, despite its rapid growth that made the city extend to a vast area, estimated at about ten kilometers by ten kilometers in each direction in the first quarter of the second century. This may have included a large area of orchards and wasteland. However, the city of Kufa witnessed turbulent historical changes, as its layout changed

---

15   Al-Amwal, pp. 291-298.

over the years, especially in the first century of the Hijra.[16] According to the recitals, it was planned five times: the first planning was in 14 AH according to the decimal system, and the second a few years later according to the septenary system. Then it was replanned a third time in the Caliphate of Uthman. The new plan aimed to make the city a field for financial investments, so the Yemeni tribes were moved away from the market area and replaced by the Thaqif tribe known for their commercial, agricultural and handicraft traditions. This planning was one of the major causes of a political revolution[17] that ended with the people of Kufa and other regions heading to the Madina, where they besieged and killed the Caliph in his home. As a result of this revolution, the city was replanned for the fourth time according to the septenary system as it was before the Caliphate of Uthman, during the reign of the fourth Caliph, Ali bin Abi Talib. It is clear that the political conflict in early Islam was closely related to the life of the new territories and attempts to monopolize commercial benefits by influential groups.

It is not easy in this field to review the basic plans for organizing the first cities and to discuss the reality of the civil divisions mentioned in historical sources such as Akhmas, Aashars, Asbaas, and Arbaas. This is because these important issues in the early history of Islam have not yet been studied, and Orientalists have tried to suggest that they are either meaningless names or just military formations unrelated to the organization of civil life, or perhaps they are borrowed from the military organization of the Romans. However, this issue can be explained by studying the overall system of the first Islamic civil government. But this takes us away from the subject at hand, and it suffices to note here that these civil organizations were based on the tribal common system that remained in the first Islamic era, which preceded the establishment of the centralized state. Every fifth area of Basra and every seventh area of Kufa represented a political administrative unit that included one tribe or a number of closely related tribes. This unit was located in a residential sector consisting of a group of housing plans around a large square that included the

---

16   Ed. Note: The Hijra (or Hijrah) refers to the Prophet Muhammad's migration (which occurred in 622 CE) from Mecca to Medina. As such, the 3rd or 4th centuries of the Hijrah take place around 900-100CE according the Western calendar.

17   Ed. Note: This is commonly known as the "First Fitna," or the First Islamic Civil War. It occurred between 656 and 661 CE.

tribe's horse barracks, local mosque, and tombs. These units were then connected to the city center, which consisted of a wide square where the central mosque was located. A strip of housing for officials, tribal chiefs and nobles separated this square, sometimes called the courtyard or the field, and they were called the people of Al-Aaliyah. The distribution of residential sectors (Fifths, Sevenths, etc.) was done fairly by drawing lots (arrows), so that one tribe was not favored over another, or the city was not used as a means of enrichment or real estate speculation. This system continued throughout the reign of Caliph Umar bin Al-Khattab and the first reign of Uthman bin Affan, but it appears that the system of tribal equality no longer suited the aspirations of the Caliph and the new governor of Kufa, Sa'id bin Al-Aas. The decision was therefore made to abandon the lottery system and plan the city within a certain tribal group and its allies in the eastern side of the city, which controlled the trade routes and market. But this attempt, as we mentioned, did not last long and ended with the revolution of the people of Kufa against the Caliphate, thus the Sevenths system was reinstated. Finally, it did not take long for it to fall under the rule of Ziyad ibn Abi Sufyan, who followed the direction of the new Umayyad state towards absolute centralization.

Ziyad made a fifth plan for Kufa and abolished the *asbaa* [system of Sevens] and replaced it with the *arbaa* [system of Quarters]. In each quarter of Kufa, he placed two equal tribes, one Yamani and the other Mudheri. He left one of the quarters as a base for central authority and restricted it to the people of Hijaz. Then, Muawiyah transferred the capital of the Iraq region to Basra and made the governor of Kufa subordinate to Ziyad. With this new political and administrative system, the system of tribal partnership (Mushtarak) was eradicated and the inhabitants were subjected to harsh measures, leading to a new division based on social class rather than lineage. This new development helped the various tribes to merge with each other, and the political conflict spread to new cities. It ended with the unification of the people of Iraq and their extensions in Khorasan[18] and the consolidation of all resistance movements into one movement that ultimately overthrew the Umayyad rule and gave birth to the Abbasid state in Kufa.

---

18   **Ed. Note:** Khorasan is located in northeastern Iran, as well as parts of present-day Afghanistan, Turkmenistan, and Uzbekistan.

3. The Fall of Islamic Communalism [Mushtarak] and the Emergence of Despotism

The emergence of despotism in Islam was linked to the liquidation of tribal communalism. We have mentioned that the Umayyad rule in Iraq implemented a new political and administrative system in the cities that relied on forcibly mixing opposing tribes to occupy them with tribal conflicts rather than confronting the new authority. Needless to say, the self-administration of tribal sectors in each city disappeared with the dominance of central authority. However, the moral status of the tribe remained, and the cities remained divided on the basis of tribal sectors, even if these sectors included tribes that were not in harmony with each other. This situation, coupled with the deepening resentment in the region against the Umayyad rule, which moved the Islamic capital from Kufa to Damascus, led to new rebellions that included various tribes and social classes, including slaves, adherents, and oppressed groups of the original inhabitants, as a growing force.

The dominance of the state over Islamic society in this stage was reflected in the transformation of the Caliphate institution from a selection process to hereditary monarchy. Since the time of Muawiya bin Abi Sufyan, the pledge of allegiance became a formal procedure aimed at securing legitimacy for the new monarchy.

Islam, for many reasons, did not adopt monarchy as a form of government. The development of the Rashidun Caliphate indicates that hereditary rule was not a known tradition in Arab leadership. Therefore, the Caliphate was established through consensus among the companions of the Prophet at the time of his death. This is evidenced by the tradition of allegiance, despite the sectarian disputes that emerged later and sought to establish hereditary rule as a pillar of Islamic religion.

The truth is that the nature of Islam as a religion and political system emerged in a society that was free from monarchy and rejected the tyranny and domination of kings. Instead, it embraced the 'democratic' tradition that was familiar to the society prior to Islam. Therefore, the Quran emphasized the *Shura* [principle of consultation] as the basis for political decision-making in several verses. The Quran was explicit in rejecting monarchy as a system of governance:

When kings enter a city, they ruin it and make the honored of its people humble...[19]

It should be noted that Islam was aware of the nature of monarchical rule, not only from the surrounding monarchical systems in Arabia but also from the monotheistic religious heritage that preceded Islam. Despite Islam's recognition of the divine nature of the Torah and Judaism as a divine law, it rejected the Jewish monarchical tradition and considered the monarchy stipulated by the Torah and ancient myths as a kind of story for people's remembrance. Therefore, wherever a kind of approval of kings appears in the Quranic verses, it is mentioned in the context of the old scriptures and not as a model for Islamic religion. It is worth mentioning that monarchy did not appear among the Quraysh, who were the highest-ranked Arabs.

The Romans and others tried to install kings in Mecca before Islam, but they failed miserably multiple times. Mecca's response was clear during the Hajj season when the Romans attempted to install one of the nobles as the king of Quraysh. One of Mecca's spokesmen said *"Inne Qurayshan laqah, la temlik wa la tumlek,"*[20] which means "Quraysh is a place of consultation, do not take over or get taken over." In Arabic, *laqah* means rejecting monarchy and advocating for leadership through consultation and selection.

The *Lisan al-Arab* dictionary defines *laqah* as "the living who do not owe allegiance to kings or have been conquered by them."

Historical sources mention that Qusayy, the assembly leader of the Quraysh tribe, took over Mecca from the Khuza'ah tribe with the help of Caesar.[21] Nonetheless, Qusayy was the one who built Dar al-Nadwa and organized the city of Mecca, dividing it into quarters and plans among the Quraysh. However, he was not a king and did not claim dictatorship over Mecca. Instead, his status rested on Quraysh's acknowledgment of him "as a leader and a just ruler," as stated by Al-Baladhuri (Ansaab al-Ashraaf 49:1).[22] There was no tradition among the Arabs of

---

19 Surah An-Naml, verse 33.

20 Jawad Ali 4:92.

21 Ibn Qutaybah: *Al-Ma'arif*, p.279.

22 Ansaab al-Ashraaf 49:1.

Hijaz, where Islam first emerged, that pushed towards monarchical rule. That's why the early Muslims were convinced of the *"Bay'ah"* (pledge of allegiance) and *"Shura"* (consultation) system. When Muawiyah tried to introduce the hereditary system, it led to the great disturbance in the Islamic state later. This is confirmed by most historians and ancient philosophers, including Ibn Rushd and Ibn Khaldun.

The abolition of the tribal communal system led, on the one hand, to the transformation of the Caliphate into an inherited monarchy and, on the other hand, to the transformation of the Islamic state into extreme centralized despotism. This is because Islam was based, as we have seen, on the old tribal traditions and extended them from the framework of a single tribe to the entire Islamic nation. This development meant that land and the main means of production became the property of the state as the representative of social authority. Therefore, the Prophet said: "The land belongs to Allah and His Messenger, then it belongs to you."[23] When the conquest of rich provinces such as Iraq and Egypt was completed, the *Kharaj* tax was imposed on the basis that it was a rent for agricultural land. We have pointed out the importance of this system and how it found its most advanced expression in the *Communist Manifesto*, but its importance here arises from its connection to the power that represents the producers. When power takes the form of a despotic system, the *Kharaj* system and state ownership of land become a solid foundation that enables tyrants to control people's lives. Despotism, as a political system, cannot arise solely from the desire of individuals to control society, because such individual desires exist in every class society and cannot become a system of government unless they have a social basis. Despotism assumes the authority of the individual over society, and this cannot be achieved without control of the social means of production, so the population becomes dependent on the state and cannot live without its consent and submission.

And this fact explains to us the ease with which modern socialist systems can deviate into a kind of modern tyranny, cloaked in the guise of 'socialism.' Without a power that represents the producers as we have said, the state that owns the means of production becomes able to exercise absolute tyranny over society. And this is what happened in Islam

---

23 Al-Amwal, p. 347.

despite its early simple beginnings and its emphasis on the principle of consultation and the subjugation of Rulers to the Ruled. Early Islam confirmed the unity of political and economic power in the state, but assumed that the state represented a society based on brotherhood in religion and participation in social wealth. However, when the Islamic Caliphate turned into a monarchy, since the time of Uthman and then into hereditary monarchy in the Umayyad period, the new political system became equipped with powers that even the most tyrannical kings in history had never dreamt of. Nevertheless, the Umayyad rule remained defined by the tribal nature of the Islamic authority, and the Umayyad Caliphs had to use their cunning as much as their zeal to suppress and execute people at times. This second aspect appeared prominently in Iraq, especially in its fierce resistance against the new Umayyad tyranny, due to the continued spirit of the Mushtarak system under which the Islamic provinces in Iraq were formed. In contrast, we see the Umayyad power more stable in Syria, where the old cities remained unchanged due to the conditions of the peace treaty, and no Islamic provinces were established there, and therefore the Mushtarak system was not known. The association of the names of the famous Islamic oppressors, such as Ziyad bin Abi Sufyan and his son Ubaidullah, and Al-Hajjaj with the rule of Iraq was due to the fierce resistance that the Umayyad regime faced in Kufa and Basra.[24]

The absolute authoritarian system in Islam integrated with the emergence of the Abbasid state. The status of tribes weakened significantly in the new state, and the army relied more on mercenaries from various classes and nationalities than on Arab tribes. The image of the new authoritarianism is clearly evident in the statements of the early Caliphs of the Abbasid dynasty. "Mansur used to say: 'I am the representative of Allah's authority on earth.'"

---

24   **Ed. Note:** Ziyad bin Abi Sufyan (622-673 CE), also known as Ziyad ibn Abihi, was appointed by Caliph Muawiya I as the governor of Basra in 665 CE and later given control over Kufa. Ubaidullah bin Ziyad (died 686 CE) was the son of Ziyad bin Abi Sufyan and served as the governor of Kufa. He is most infamous for his role in the Battle of Karbala in 680 CE, where he ordered the killing of Husayn ibn Ali, the grandson of the Prophet Muhammad. Al-Hajjaj bin Yusuf (661-714 CE) was a powerful and controversial governor under the Umayyad Caliphate, appointed as the governor of Iraq in 694 CE. He is remembered for his administrative reforms and brutal suppression of revolts, which made him both an effective ruler and a feared enforcer. These figures are associated with the harsh enforcement of Umayyad rule in Iraq during periods of significant resistance and unrest.

The authoritarian system in Islam assumes organized government management of the economy as long as the state is the owner of the means of production. This led to the organization of *diwans* [administrative departments] and the development of administrative and mathematical sciences, in addition to the emergence of the executioner and astrologer among the prominent Caliphate officials.

What gives Islam's authoritarianism its unique features is its tendency towards capitalist development on the one hand and its conflict with its historical roots, which are not based on authoritarianism, on the other. The Abbasid system developed production to a high degree and organized the industry on new foundations that the world had not seen before. It introduced advanced methods in agriculture and transportation, enabling the growth of major cities such as Baghdad, Samarra, Kufa, and Basra, some of which at times had populations of up to two million or more, such as Baghdad in the third century AH.[25]

With the development of economic production, *diwans* evolved. Some of the ancient writers said, "The circulation of money, its continuity, increase, and abundance, all depend on these *diwans*." The same writer also mentions statements indicating the importance of mathematics in the Islamic 'bureaucratic' system, saying, "The pivot of the kingdom depends on accounting."

During the Abbasid era, the state became a collective capitalist that exploited all the territories under the Islamic Caliphate. With the development of global trade, which expanded to include the known world at that time, industrial production institutions such as textiles, factories, markets, and banking grew. The population of the cities grew to the point where traditional agriculture was no longer able to meet their food needs and the demands of the industries for raw materials. Baghdad became a huge center for the production of various types of fabric, especially cotton, as well as expensive silk textiles. All of this led to a new need for raw materials and new sources of precious metals to cover the need for commercial exchange tools. These developments were associated with a disruption of the previous relationship between the state and the cities. In Islam, the state used to initiate the creation of new cities and plan them, then provide them with livelihoods and food through

---

25   Ed. Note: Equivalent to 816 - 913 CE in Western calendars.

the policy of *Kharaj* and conquests. With the development of civil industrial production and the growth of markets, and the contraction of conquests, the state turned towards doubling the internal exploitation of the workers and imposing taxes on traders and markets, and then soon entered as a partner in economic institutions through the *Waqf* system and guarantees. Finally, the state began seizing senior officials and ministers and confiscating the property of the wealthy. All of this led to a deepening of the contradiction between the city and the state.

This tense relationship between the state and the capital city can be observed at a glance by examining the design of the circular city of Baghdad. This city was designed as a fortress with intersecting inner walls separated by massive iron gates. The inhabitants themselves were used as human barriers against any attempt to infiltrate the city, and the entire city was surrounded by a moat and forged gates. In addition to these physical fortifications, the Caliph's astronomers derived celestial fortifications by making each wall of the walls represent a planet of the seven stars, and the Caliph's palace was made the center of this miniature universe, where the Abbasid kings were seated, like gods in the sky. The Caliph did not stop at these fortifications; he also divided the city into independent sectors that could be isolated from one another, as well as each alley in the Round City—all equipped with secure gates and limited entry points that were easy to monitor and close off.

This urban system, as clearly shown, is in stark contrast to the design of the early Islamic cities—as open cities without walls or gates. It becomes clear, therefore, that the Caliphate has become living in a state of fear and suspicion of the civilian population, and that the entire political system has become based on tyranny and oppression.

The clash between the state and the city was also accompanied by a transformation of the role of the army. The first Muslims were the fighters, and therefore there was no distinction between the army and the inhabitants of the first Islamic cities of Muslims. Then this situation changed somewhat when the Umayyad state was established, which faced growing resistance from the people of Iraq, and was forced to rely on the soldiers of the Levant, and then these soldiers were withdrawn and a fortified city was established for them to be away from the anger of the people of Iraq. For this reason, the city of Wasit was built, which remained called the camp or the palace for a period of time, the palace means the great fortress. With the establishment of the Abbasid state, as we mentioned, the position of the tribes in the new state faded, and the army became professional soldiers in addition to the volunteers who joined military campaigns and then returned to their civilian lives afterwards. This system led to an increasing cohesion between the general population and the soldiers, making it difficult for the Caliphate to use them against the city dwellers. Therefore, the Abbasid Caliphs turned to using slaves in their army and preferred those who did not speak the language of the city dwellers to live in complete isolation from the people. This policy began with Al-Mansur's purchase and use of slaves, and then expanded during Al-Ma'mun's reign when he felt the danger of the general population as a political and military force and the influence of the Khurasani soldiers on them. The friction between the general population and the Turkish slaves reached the point of bloody clashes, forcing Al-Mu'tasim to leave Baghdad and establish Samarra as a large military camp and administrative center where the Caliphate could be fortified.

It is well known that the consequences of this policy were the Mamluks monopolizing power and turning the Caliphs into tools devoid of authority, appointed and removed by the Mamluks at will. This dominance of the military over the state led to the ruin of the entire country and eventually to opening its doors to occupiers and invaders. Thus, the state transformed into a parasitic institution that oppressed society and plundered the labor of the toilers.

Thus, the Islamic Caliphate entered a phase of decline and deterioration, with its economic role and moral status fading among the different sectors of the Islamic society. This became apparent after the Caliphate's return from Samarra to Baghdad, where the Caliphs engaged in the confiscation of ministers and merchants, then handed over Baghdad to adventurers from the Daylam and Turkish military. These adventurers proceeded to inflame sectarian animosities and religious conflicts to tighten their control over the country. As a result of these circumstances, the occupiers encouraged the emergence of jurisprudential schools that justified despotism and turned the people into docile cows that produced milk for the rulers. A new style of flattery and incense burning for tyrants emerged, which the Seljuk minister called the "night armies" who fought to keep the sultans in power and humiliate the people. However, this development in despotism and the decline of the Caliphate did not come in isolation from the rise of popular movements.

4. The Emergence of the Call for a New Mushtarak

SPONTANEOUS MOVEMENTS

By spontaneous movements, we mean the popular and armed resistance movements that aimed at returning to the first Islam or to the old religions and laws, such as the Babak movement,[26] for example. This does not mean that these movements did not have ideas to guide them, but rather that these goals were understood within the framework of traditional societies. The movements that we call spontaneous did not have a conscious understanding of the social transformations brought about by Islam, and therefore did not understand their new historical tasks. They simply followed the spirit of resistance against tyrannical rule without providing a new social alternative that corresponded to the new circumstances.

At first, the signs of these movements appeared negatively, rejecting participation in the responsibilities of the Caliphate and state because such participation meant contributing to the oppression of the subjects and contradicting the teachings of Islam as understood by those who believed in following the first Islamic law. There were a significant number of jurists and ascetics who were imprisoned or killed in trying to persuade them to accept the position of judgeship or political leadership. Examples of these include Abu Hanifa, Sufyan al-Thawri, and Al-Fadl ibn Bazwan al-Adwani, who was beheaded by Al-Hajjaj because he refused political assignment.[27] Similarly, we see negative resistance among many of the early ascetics, whose praying against the Caliphs of evil is repeated in historical texts. These calls were not just religious emotions that desired isolation and worship, but also expressed the anger of the

---

26 **Ed. Note:** The Babak Khorramdin movement, often referred to as the Babak Movement, was a significant uprising against the Abbasid Caliphate in the early Islamic period. The movement is named after its leader, Babak Khorramdin, who led the rebellion from 816 to 837 CE.

27 Ibn Qutaybah: 'Uyun al-Akhbar 210:2.

masses against the despotic state. It is easy to detect a democratic spirit and revolutionary trend in the words of many of them, such as the statement attributed to Sadif bin Maimun, a slave of the Banu Hashim, who said:

> O Allah, our wealth has become in circulation among few instead of sharing, and our leadership has become dominant instead of by consultation. Our covenant has become an inheritance instead of a nation's choice. The amusement and musical instruments have been bought with the money of the orphan and widow. The Muslims have been ruled over by the people of the covenant. In each district, the most corrupt people had carried out their affairs. O Allah, as the injustice is ready to be harvested... So, release a harvesting hand from the Rightness, to disperse Its unity, drown their sound, so that the truth may shine in its best form and its most perfect light.[28]

It is worth noting that the prayers of the ascetics were not effective against tyrants, and that material oppression could only be fought with swords, not noble emotions alone. This was understood by the Khawarij, who were known for their strict adherence to religion and piety, and called themselves *Ash-Shurat* [the sellers] because they traded the worldly life for the hereafter.[29] The Khawarij followed a confrontational approach with the Caliphate and gathered various groups of laborers, artisans, Bedouins, and those resentful of the state. They specifically protested against the Quraysh's monopoly on power and believed that the Caliphate was permissible for the Quraysh and others, as long as the nation agreed to their election. The Khawarij were known for their bravery and disregard for life in the pursuit of piety. They shook the thrones of more than one Caliph and tyrant, but were unable to provide a real alternative that could unite opponents of tyranny. Furthermore, their practical approach was somewhat parasitic, as they saw the collection of tribute and seizure of property as their right without considering the rights of the toilers. As a result, their movement was limited to fringe factions in society and did not form a historical alternative to the increasing tyranny and capitalism under the Caliphate.

During the Abbasid era, the cities became the major social power that threatened the Caliphate. The toilers of Baghdad emerged during the war between Al-Amin and Al-Ma'mun as a military force that was

---

28 Ibn Qutaybah: Uyun al-Akhbar 94:2.

29 Quran 4:74 and 9:111.

more powerful and steadfast than the Caliphate's armies. They organized themselves and continued to resist Al-Ma'mun's army even after the collapse of the Baghdad Caliphate and the dispersal of its mercenaries. The popular resistance continued for a long time after the entry of Al-Ma'mun's army, and a popular militia was formed in the markets of Baghdad, which took it upon themselves to guard the markets and suppress thieves. However, as a spontaneous movement, it could not sustain its high revolutionary spirit, and the Caliphate was eventually able to disperse it after a period of time.

The weakness revealed by the civil war and the Ayārrīn uprising in Baghdad had profound echoes throughout the entire Abbasid state. Some historical sources attribute the explosion of the Babak movement in Azerbaijan to the events in Baghdad and the Ayārrīn revolution (Ibn Qutaybah: *Al-Ma'arif*, 170). The Babak movement called for adherence to ancient common traditions and resistance to the armies of the Caliphate that displaced people from their lands and turned their areas into fields for capitalist investment, especially in the search for precious metals and for the private pastures of the Baghdad Caliph. The Babak movement lasted for more than twenty years and established a unique social model based on shared ownership and the selection of leaders. Babak was the leader of this revolutionary movement that shook the Abbasid state, he was a simple daily wage worker herding animals. His father had come to Azerbaijan from Al-Madā'in seeking a livelihood. The movement established some cities and military strongholds and threatened the armies of the Caliphs, leaving an indelible mark that the laborers could follow in rebelling against injustice and oppression. We see this influence in the cautious allusions to this movement in the writings of contemporary thinkers who were aware of its reality. Al-Ma'arri describes it with caution and ambiguity, saying:

> Babak opened the door to tyranny and found among the worst of the followers. And I think his struggle... the best-known struggle.[30]

And the movement of the Bābakīyah was followed by a wider and more dangerous movement on the Caliphate, which was the *Zanj* [slave] rebellion in Basra in the mid-third century. The leader of this movement was in Samarra when Bābak was crucified there, but it is not known

---

30   Risalat Al-Ghufran, p. 490.

precisely how much he was influenced by it. However, the traditions of the Khawārij were clearer in their teachings and the few traces that have reached us about it. It was also influenced by the Zaydīyah movement that appeared in Baghdad and Kufa at the time, led by Yahya ibn Umar al-Zaydī, which received widespread support from the residents of Baghdad at the time, as we can see in Ibn al-Rūmī's famous poem that begins:

> Look ahead, consider which path you will follow
>
> Two paths, one straight and one crooked

The owner of the *Zanj* was initially a teacher of children in Samarra, but he became indignant with his share of life, which he called "the craft of the infirm." Verses are narrated about him that reveal his social aspirations, as he says:

> O craft of the Infirm, you are close to death
>
> Do I have any salvation from you, can I be reunited with my family?
>
> If myself is content with teaching children
>
> At the mercy of fate, I will be content with humiliation
>
> Can a free man be content with teaching children
>
> Who thought that the means of living are very wide on the earth?

As for the *Zanj* who revolted, they were slaves used in inhumane conditions to clear swamps and reclaim land for intensive agricultural investment. Basra was a center for the growth of this type of intensive agricultural investment system for growing cotton, sugar cane, palm trees, and fruits, according to the system of private disinheritance. The use of *Zanj* was, in fact, an extension of the agricultural system in the Arabian Peninsula before and after Islam, as many historical accounts and recent excavations in Syria confirm.

However, the *Zanj* Rebellion demonstrated patterns of civil and military organization unknown to earlier revolts. They established commercial cities and leveraged global maritime trade, which threatened the Abbasid Caliphate in Baghdad. They also minted their own currency and emphasized the brotherhood of all elements of the rebellion regardless of race and color. The movement lasted for fourteen years before the Caliphate managed to defeat the rebels, destroy their cities, and disperse their forces. The reasons for the rebellion's failure were not limited to the superiority of the Caliphate's armies and their military technology, but also included the nature of the movement itself. It did not receive widespread support from city dwellers, who viewed the *Zanj* as their enemies. Additionally, the movement did not recognize that the system of slavery was the cause of the enslavement of those wretched *Zanj*. The leader of the *Zanj* continued to promise the rebels ownership of slaves!

Following the *Zanj* revolution, a larger and different revolutionary movement emerged: the Qarmatian movement. This movement began in the countryside of Kufa. This area was based on capitalist agriculture and wage labor, not on the labor of the slaves as was the case in Basra. The biggest capitalists in the Kufa region was a military official who worked in financial dealings in Baghdad. He then undertook to finance the Caliphate for a few years when the treasury went bankrupt, and this trader earned huge profits as he gave himself the right to collect taxes as a redemption of his loan to the Caliphate treasury. The sparks of the Qarmatian revolution were against this greedy capitalist, so the peasants of the countryside and the workers of Kufa rose up in their region, and it did not take long for it to spread to most of the '*Sawad*' (i.e., the countryside of Iraq). The movement also found growing support among the urban laborers, especially in Baghdad. One of the most important accomplishments of the Qarmatian movement was the establishment of communal cities. They established their base in a city they built themselves, called Dar al-Hijra, and built walls around it. They then shared all their possessions and tools. The movement continued for several years until the Caliphate was able to scatter and destroy their cities in the Arabian Peninsula. However, the Qarmatian movement was better organized than previous spontaneous movements and more aware of the superiority of the Caliphate's armies, so they planned to move their base to a secure location far from the grasp of the Baghdad Caliphate. They succeeded in establishing the Qarmatian state in the Bahrain area and made the city of Al-Hajr their capital. Historical accounts and the observations of ancient travelers who visited and witnessed their organization indicate that they operated on a system of communal cooperation and shared wealth. The Qarmatians' awareness of the political and military situation they lived in is confirmed by what Al-Ma'arri said about them: "Their grandfather advised them to stay on this land (Hajr and Al-Ahsa) to keep it away from the sultans."[31]

The Qarmatians used sophisticated military techniques that allowed them to defeat armies several times their size. It appears that they used gunpowder, as inferred from some accounts, to intimidate their enemies in battles. One of the most significant achievements of the Qarmatian movement was the establishment of a new political system that did not involve tyranny and oppression.[32] Leadership among them was based on elections, and in their later periods, they formed a council to govern the state. They abolished physical punishments such as imprisonment and torture for those who violated social norms and laws. Instead, they punished offenders by assigning them to work as shepherds for sheep and camels or making the culprit beg in the town.

The movement of the Qarmatians left a profound impact on the popular and intellectual movements of their era, some of which can be seen in the Enlightenment philosophers and thinkers' calls for the abolition of the state, private property, and brotherhood among human beings. However, this movement was secret and persecuted, and those accused of it were subjected to various forms of torture and punishment, making it difficult to measure its impact from the historical texts we have.

As for the origins of the Qarmatian movement, it appears to have been an extension of the agricultural traditions of the Mesopotamian valley, nourished and deepened by the spirit of Islamic rebellion and ancient communism that Muslims had brought to Iraq. However, it quickly folded under the influence of the Ismaili movement, although the latter differed fundamentally from the Qarmatian movement. Historians of old and modern times often confuse the two movements because of their overlap in a period. The Qarmatian movement was based on the traditions of participation, cooperation, and the belief in the election of leaders, which was not the case in Ismaili teachings. Therefore, the two movements clashed later in violent conflict clashes that led to the Fatimid state's displacement from 'Africa' (north Africa) to Egypt and the building of Cairo, as recorded in ancient history books.

---

31   Zajr al-Nabih, p.81.

32   Refer to what Al-Maqrizi mentioned in his book *I'tiadh al-Hunafa* Vol. 1, p. 203, and compare it with p. 33 of the Cairo edition of 1967.

The Qarmatian movement contributed to the emergence of a great intellectual and philosophical movement witnessed in the fourth century AH[33] and integrated with the deepening crisis of the Caliphate and the establishment of the Fatimid state in Egypt.

THE EMERGENCE OF THE THEORY OF AL-MUSHTARAK

The intellectual life in Islam witnessed a remarkable flourishing after the establishment of Baghdad, which was the meeting point of world civilizations and the gathering place of thinkers, doctors, astrologers, and scientists from various horizons. The general literary trends were deeply rooted in various philosophical elements that were nurtured by translations from other languages, as well as the need of the capitalist state's economy for science and mathematics. Some intellectual schools had been inclined towards defending the interests of the toilers and confronting the despotic system since early periods. As the crisis of the Islamic state deepened and revolutionary movements emerged, and the conditions of intellectuals deteriorated in general, many elements among the top philosophers, doctors, and poets found themselves detached or distant from high officials, and closer to the situation of the persecuted public. They began to feel the bitterness of the political and social conditions' decline, and saw themselves increasingly alienated from the existing society.

However, these thinkers did not stop at the boundaries of complaint, but rather wielded their pens as a drawn swords against social injustice, political tyranny, and the myths propagated by the rulers' servants. This criticism reached a degree that frightened the Caliphate, to the extent that Al-Mu'tamid issued an order banning philosophy books in 279 AH, as mentioned by Al-Tabari:

> ...the booksellers were made to swear not to sell books of Faith Discussions, Argument, and Philosophy.[34]

Doctors and intellectuals began to view society not with indifference, but rather as an ailing condition that must be treated by changing the conditions of the public. Al-Razi wrote his famous book *The Spiri-*

---

33   **Ed. Note:** 912 to 1009 CE.

34   History 2131:3.

tual Medicine to emphasize this trend that had spread among a number of intellectual schools. In the view of Al-Razi, society, like the human body, can become sick and can be treated with medicines and cures to regain its health and well-being. The cure for the disease of society, in his view, was in establishing proper social rules and then changing the general morality through education and philosophy. Therefore, he believed that the foundations of misery in society were based on monopolizing wealth and the dependence of the ruling classes on exploiting the labor of producers, and he saw work as the origin of wealth, saying:

> Philosophers have not considered anyone rich except through industries, not through possessions.[35]

Al-Razi had a comprehensive theory about the world, including time, space, and ethics. He wrote a book criticizing prophecies and religions, which had a wide impact in his time and in medieval Europe. Al-Razi believed that the essence of human life is living freely without exploitation or pain. He developed an ethical theory based on the nature of pleasure, arguing that pleasure and pain are related to the state of nature. Pleasure is the return from an unnatural state to a natural state, while pain is the opposite. Therefore, he believed that the best behavior for humans is to live modestly, so as not to exhaust oneself with greed and not to subject oneself to slavery to others. Al-Razi defined money as a 'symbol' indicating the value of work, making it easier for people to exchange goods and services. He argued that gold and other precious metals have no intrinsic value, their value comes from human labor. He urged philosophers and thinkers to stay away from rulers and encouraged them to teach the public to 'purify themselves' of ignorance through philosophy. He said:

> The soul cannot be purified from the impurities of this world or freed to that (upper) world except by studying philosophy... If the common people, who destroyed themselves and neglected researching, had looked at it with the slightest glance, then this will be their salvation from this impurity, even though they might realize a little of it.[36]

Al-Razi believed that everyone was capable of understanding philosophy, so he did not accept the division of society into a distinguished

---

35   Rasa'il al-Razi, p. 84.

36   Ibid., p. 302.

elite with superior minds and a common people with lower minds and souls, as described by the Sultan's commentary. When a theologian objected to Al-Razi's statements and asked him in disbelief, "Do people have equal intelligence, ambition, and sagacity?" Al-Razi replied,

> If they exerted themselves and worked on what concerns them, they would be equal in ambition and intelligence.[37]

From his statements, it becomes clear that one of the reasons for the general population's misfortune is their ignorance of the realities of things and their falling victim to the deception of religious leaders. Al-Razi called for the necessity of human cooperation and for reason to be the guide to human actions and social relationships. Therefore, he criticized religious laws because they created animosity between people who were better off without them. Al-Razi opposed Aristotle's philosophy from the perspective that it was a support for logicians in justifying religious thought and sectarian conflicts.

Philosophical schools that opposed Al-Razi's naturalistic school have emerged, based on Aristotle's heavenly conception of existence. It is known that Aristotle's philosophy contains elements that were incompatible with religious thought, as he conceived of God as a mere first mover in eternal existence.

The divine philosophers remedied this issue by adopting the modern Platonic thought and attributing it to Aristotle, saying that the universe is composed of a number of interlocking spherical layers with the Logos in the center who overflows by its nature onto the existence. From it, other celestial entities derive their levels of nobility, descending toward the world of corruption under the moon zodiac.

In the face of the naturalistic and idealistic schools influenced by the followers of Aristotle, a third school attempted to reconcile the two, targeting the creation of a new philosophy that could unify the scattered intellectual schools and pave the way for the salvation of society from oppression, by adopting the modern Platonism and the direction of the unity. This third school was represented by Al-Farabi, who attempted in his book *The Harmonization of the Opinions of the Two Sages* to present a new philosophy with internal coherence, based on the positions of

---

37   Ibid., p. 296.

both Aristotle and Plato simultaneously. Al-Farabi's main goal was to propose a virtuous social and political alternative to the despotic state, and therefore, the virtuous city was the axis around which his most important philosophical works revolved.

For Al-Farabi, the virtuous city was influenced by the Platonic Republic, but it differed from it fundamentally, as it was an idealized city that *could* be realized in this world, even if its realization was distant. Al-Farabi launched from the era in which he lived and not from the narrow horizons of the Greek city-state, and thus imagined the existence of a virtuous globe consisting of virtuous nations and virtuous cities, the latter of which were composed of shops, roads, and individual houses. However, the virtuous city formed the virtuous social unit between the global level and the small household unit. It is known that this global concept, which Al-Farabi proposed, exceeded the limits of ancient Greek thought and reflected the unity of the global market that emerged after Islam. Just as Al-Razi envisioned society as a sick human being, Al-Farabi likened the city to the human body as an interconnected organic unit whose parts are subject to every unifier.

Among the bold ideas that Al-Farabi proposed was the possibility of establishing collective leadership at the top of the virtuous city, as he saw the necessity of the extraordinary merits In the virtuous leader, which is only available to the prophets. Therefore, he said that it was possible to provide these merits and conditions through a number of leaders who cooperate with each other to manage the virtuous city.

Al-Farabi distinguished between the virtuous city and the other cities which he called *Jahiliyah* [pre-Islamic] cities. He said that some of these cities are bad, like the city of 'domination' (tyranny) and the city of 'villenage' meaning cities based on wealth and physical pleasures. There were also good *Jahiliyah* cities, such as the 'collective city' of which he said:

> It is the one that its people intended to be free, where each one works as he wishes, and their desires are not hindered in anything at all.[38]

Although this description refers to Greek cities mentioned in the writings of Aristotle and Plato, it is actually closer to the concept of the

---

38   Al-Farabi, *The Opinions of the People of the Virtuous City*, p. 133.

pre-Islamic urban commonality, especially in Mecca. Al-Farabi then clarifies the features of pre-Islamic cities and their share of commonality and cooperation, saying that some people from those cities believed that: "Participation in birth from one parent is his connection to him, and by this they come together, unite, and balance themselves to overcome others..."[39]

Others believed:

> Participation in reproduction, that is, the male of this group breeds with the females of the other group... through intermarriage.

Then some others saw that:

> The connection is in the participation of the first leader who gathered and organized them until they overcame others and obtained the best of the benefits of ignorance [Al-Jahiliyah].[40]

Then he says:

> Some people saw the connection as being through oaths, alliances, and covenants, based on what each person can contribute... and they become united to overcome others...

Others saw the connection as being through:

> Similarity in character and natural disposition, and participation in language and tongue... and this is for every nation. They should love each other and oppose those who are not like them, for nations differ in these three aspects.[41]

Al-Farabi here clearly demonstrates the emergence of the nationalist tendency and the formation of nations based on national interest in overcoming other nations. It is evident from his political and social analysis of "ignorant" cities, that he contradicts such narrow boundaries and calls for a virtuous world. Later, Al-Farabi presented a picture of the common city and said:

> Others believed that the connection is in the participation in the house, then in the houses, and that the most important of them is the participation in the house, then in the path, then in the neighborhood. That is why they support their neighbor, for the neighbor is the participant in the path and in the

---

39   Ibid., p. 154.
40   Ibid., p. 155.
41   Ibid.

neighborhood, then the participation in the area in which the city is located.[42]

After this review of the social models of cities and the unique characteristics of each model, Al-Farabi returns to the Virtuous City to confirm its superiority over these models. He says that:

> ...the people of the Virtuous City have common ranks and things they know and do, and other things related to knowledge and work that belong to each rank and each individual among them. But each one of them only becomes happy in two things: the common one that belongs to him and the others together, and the one that belongs to the rank they are in.[43]

Al-Farabi believes that the Virtuous City should be like the human body, where the organs and components are differentiated according to the role they play in the whole. And according to him, this differentiation should be based on the natural predisposition of each individual, not on domination and power. It is clear that this social model proposed by Al-Farabi reflected the highest concept in Islamic society in the fourth century of the Hijri era. At that time, traders and scholars aspired to high social ranks that were not provided to them by the existing tyrannical system, the ranks in which the whole economic, civic, and intellectual development in that era was heading towards them.

The globalization that characterized Islam from the beginning, and the subsequent development in the global market, the growth of links between distant societies, and the formation of multiple nationalities cities, all led to the aspiration for a free global society that included the known world at that time. This society provided means for global cooperation and liberation from systems of tyranny and domination by armies and conquerors.

It is known that Al-Farabi's theory contradicted the individual despotism of the Abbasid Caliphate system, so this theory did not pass without being attacked and criticized by some contemporary philosophers of Al-Farabi who remained influenced by the model of despotism. Abu Hassan al-Amiri criticized the theory of 'collective presidency' that Al-Farabi proposed, referring to him as belonging to "the Juvenile Philosophers." Al-Amiri, as it appears, was influenced by the style of royal despotism and he mixed up Sapor bin Ardeshir and Plato to support

---

42   Ibid., pp. 155-156.

43   Ibid., p. 134.

his theory of monopolizing the presidency. In a chapter entitled "Is it permissible for one presidency to be organized with two presidents?" he said:

> Some of the Juvenile Philosophers said that when all the qualities of goodness do not meet in one president, then it is necessary to establish the presidency between two people, one of whom is wise and has no power to rule, and the other has the power to rule. Similarly, this applies to a group, and the whole of them may act as one president through cooperation. Abu Hassan said that: what this man (i.e. Al-Farabi) said has no meaning, and it is not permissible for there to be more than one head, but rather the presidency is by opinion (vision), so whoever has no opinion (vision) does not deserve the presidency. If there is a wise person with no power, the way to deal with him is to appoint him as the president, then the strong person acts as his deputy in matters, referring to his opinion in small and large matters. If the presidency was monopolized by the strong, he would rule like a minister or a counselor. This may be permissible. But a presidency held by two people without one being under the other, this is something meaningless at all. Aristotle said that it is incumbent upon the king to fear the one who is fit for his position, and to keep him away and be cautious. This is the way for everything that cannot have two people. Abu Hassan said that he has made it clear that there cannot be two Rulers. Allah Almighty said: "If there were gods in them (heaven and earth) except Allah, then they would have perished." Sapor bin Ardeshir said, "Just as Reign cannot be fit for partnership, neither can opinion be fit for isolation."[44]

This indicates that the disagreement revolves around two different issues. Al-Farabi did not intend to solidify royal rule but to abolish it and establish a society based on choice rather than domination. As for Al-Amiri, he pointed out the inappropriateness of participating in royal rule and his statement is correct from the perspective of the interests of despots.

This same disagreement took place between Al-Tawhidi and Meskewaih in their dialogue *Al-Hawamil wa Al-Shawamil* when Al-Tawhidi asked: "Why do people say there is no good in partnership? This appears to be true because we have not seen a stable Reign, or a successful affair, or a successful agreement in partnership." Meskewaih answered:

> Partnership for a person is not reprehensible in all cases, but it is reprehensible in things that others may rely on and monopolize its possibilities, such as writing and other professions. As for matters that one person cannot com-

---

44 Abu Hassan al-Amiri: Al-Sa'adah wal-As'ad, pp. 194-196.

plete alone, and no one can rely on alone, partnership is obligatory, such as the possibility of loading a millstone, freighting large ships, and other industries that are done by large groups and through partnership and cooperation.

Partnership is indicative of the weakness of the partners, it will flawed and corrupt later the shared matter compared to what can be done alone, even if humans are excused in some and not in others.

As for human Ruling, since it is one of the things that are organized by one management and one order—even if groups participate in it, they proceed from a single opinion and become like machines for the king—the majority is united, and good order appears. Therefore, despotism is undoubtedly better, as we have shown previously.[45]

So, participation in production is good, but despotism is better for governance. The disagreement here is between two opposing theories of despotism and statehood, and Al-Tawhidi does not express his opinion but rather raises the question. However, we can understand the perspectives of both Meskewaih and Al-Amiri on the freedom of society, where Al-Amiri sees, for example,

Rulers and slavery are two names that confirm each other... as if they are two names that confirm the same meaning, for Rulers need slaves, and the slaves need Rulers.[46]

And this exact perspective is what Al-Farabi intended to refute and call for a society based on natural readiness of individuals, as he saw it. Therefore, Al-Farabi did not allocate a place for kings in the virtuous city, but rather called the cities that were subject to the kings 'cities of conquest' and 'cities of meanness.'

In general, new theories emerged in Islam in the third and fourth centuries AH (9th to 10th century CE) calling for the removal of the system of tyranny and the establishment of a new political-social system based on choice, not domination; and participation in ownership and cooperation in earning. Ironically, Al-Amieri, after saying what he said about the necessity of tyranny in politics, goes back and supports Plato's views on participation, citing the latter as saying:

The basis of friendship is raising the right hand (i.e., ownership) and sharing, and this is because calamity and corruption only arise from exclusivity in blessings and delight. Therefore, each person in the city must realize that

---

45   Al-Hawamil wa Al-Shawamil, pp. 64-66.

46   Al-Amiri, *Happiness and Making Happy*, p. 208.

his care and wealth should not be limited to his family and children, but it is obligatory for what each person has in his hand to be available to others when they need it for themselves, their family, or their children... and it should be prevented from saying, "This is mine, and that is yours." According to what we said, the people of the city should participate in necessary and beneficial matters to become like one body, if one of them suffers, the other suffers...[47]

THE BRETHREN OF PURITY [IKHWAN AL-SAFA] MOVEMENT

The Brotherhood of Purity movement emerged in the aftermath of the intellectual movement established by the advanced generation of thinkers such as Al-Razi and Al-Farabi during a major revolutionary crisis that took place in the second half of the fourth century AH. The Brotherhood of Purity adopted much of their social and civic philosophy from Al-Farabi, and made semi-clear references to him in their letters. They also adopted Al-Razi's doctrine of pleasure and pain, although they abandoned his natural views on time, place, and religious laws. However, the Brotherhood of Purity was more advanced than its earlier generation of philosophers and thinkers. It did not confine its horizons to scriptural teachings and the preaching of a philosophical view of the world, but went beyond that to political organization and planning to topple the Caliphate system. In other words, it was a revolutionary movement with the most precise organization that began to spread its ideas in a simple and influential way, and in a style that revolutionary movements had not yet realized until this era, in terms of linking scientific knowledge to the political movement.

The origins of this movement can be traced back to the late Umayyad period, as evident from its first generation of representatives which appeared in Basra in the early Abbasid era. Among them were Ibn al-Muqaffa and Salih ibn Abd al-Qados, as well as a group of poets and thinkers, whom Al-Jahidh mentioned in some of his writings. The movement that disseminated the Epistles of the Brethren of Purity draws some of its origins from the first movement, but it differs from it in terms of methodology and content. This new movement emerged after the Fatimids moved from Africa [Tunisia] and established the city of

---

47   Ibid., p. 247.

Cairo in 362 AH, which had a great impact on the entire Islamic world at that time. The Abbasid Caliphate was shaken, and fear dominated the Dailamites who were occupying Baghdad and the real power brokers in Iraq, while the Byzantines took advantage of the confusion that prevailed in the Caliphate and attacked a number of Islamic cities, captured their people, and destroyed what they could not keep. The reaction to these attacks was significant among the population. The people of the frontier towns adjacent to Aleppo and Mosul marched to Baghdad demanding that the Caliphate assist them and repel the attacks on the frontiers. This march quickly developed into a large popular uprising. The people of Baghdad attacked the Caliphate palace and burned some of its outskirts. Then the movement of the Al-Ayyarin and the Al-A'urat who took control of Baghdad for a period of time reemerged. The Dailamites forces withdrew to their positions after failing to repel the uprising, and the real power in Baghdad fell into the hands of the Al-Ayyarin, who formed their own forces and organizations. The inhabitants of the neighborhoods and their leaders joined them, demanding that the officials defend the state against foreign invasions and address the demands of the poor. They then sent a delegation to the Dailami governor, presenting their demands and saying, "there is no obedience if he does not fulfill their demands."

When the Dailamites and Turks, who were in control of affairs, were unable to suppress the masses, they began to incite sectarian conflicts. They sent troops to burn down the markets in Karkh (western part of Baghdad) and then pitted one sect against another in order to focus on eliminating everyone. One contemporary historian of those events said:

> The system was scattered, the sultan was humiliated, and the animosity between these two classes regarding religion and worldly matters emerged, whereas it was only regarding religion before.[48]

However, igniting the flames of sectarian conflict did not save the rulers. They became divided among themselves, and a war broke out between the Dailamites and Turkish troops, which ended with the occupation of Baghdad by A'dhud al-Dawlah in 364 AH. This adventurer was ambitious and wanted to make Baghdad the capital of a new sprawling empire. He therefore began to eliminate all opposition political and

---

48   Miskawayh's *Experiences of Nations*, p. 32.

religious forces, arresting the leaders of the religious movement and exiling them to Fars, disarming the public and spreading spies everywhere, so that even school teachers would entice children to report on their fathers. A'dhud al-Dawlah tried to transfer the Caliphate to his sons when he persuaded the Caliph to marry his daughter, and he arrested prominent thinkers such as Al-Sabi and others. He befriended astrologers and asked them to show the signs of the stars in favor of his state and appeared in the form of brutish despots.

When the resources of the Abbasid state were exhausted, he resorted to confiscating private industrial institutions such as water mills, monopolizing the silk and ice industries, and imposing heavy taxes on markets. As a result of this policy, a movement emerged among the people of Baghdad and the Iraqi cities calling for the unification of all sects, religions, and unions to expel the invaders and conquerors. In this atmosphere, the Brotherhood of Purity declared itself and spread its messages among the people through the scribes.

The Brethren of Purity called for the unity of hearts and a pure brotherhood free from selfish desires in order to serve the community as a whole. They found in the philosophy of Al-Farabi the closest ideas that express their goals in the necessity of unifying partial souls into one through philosophy and adherence to virtuous ethics. They said, the same as Al-Razi and Al-Farabi believed, that the society is sick and all religions are sick, and there is no way to purify them from ignorance except through Greek philosophy. This idea was expressed by Al-Farabi in his book.[49] However, the Brethren of Purity went further than Al-Farabi in their idealism and said that the source of all evils is nature, and that man is composed of body and soul, with the body being the source of evils while the soul is a pure heavenly essence that can be corrupted by ignorance and indulgence in bodily pleasures. Therefore, their ethical philosophy focused on the necessity of purifying man from the "filth of nature." This led them to prioritize education and spreading awareness among people in their revolutionary work, and they disseminated their messages for this purpose. They did not limit their teachings to one school of thought, but rather tried to unify the different and sometimes conflicting directions into one ideal current, saying:

---

49   Al-Farabi, *The Opinions of the People of the Virtuous City*, p. 140.

Our brothers, may Allah support them, should not oppose any science or abandon any book, nor should they be biased towards any school of thought because our opinion and school of thought encompass all schools and unite all sciences...[50]

Needless to say, such an approach involved an attempt to leap over contradictions and walk on the path of selection from different schools that aligned with their unifying goal. Such a direction cannot succeed as long as it lacks internal unity and coherence within its intellectual system. The Brethren of Purity emphasized the importance of spiritual matters and mastering "the science of psychology," and instead of the earthly virtuous city, they called for a "spiritually virtuous city," saying: "[s]houldn't the construction of this city be on earth?"[51] because it would be polluted by nature and the unjust cities that exist around it.

Nevertheless, for various reasons, they began to preach astrology, claiming that a certain astrological conjunction indicated the rise of the State of the Brethren of Purity, and urged their followers to prepare for this great event. However, when the conjunction occurred and their state did not materialize, their claims were exposed as false to the people. Al-Ma'arri sarcastically remarked about them:

> You hoped for an imam in the misleading conjunction,
>
> But when it passed, you postponed it to later years.

Ironically, they had condemned astrology in some of their epistles, where they stated through the voice of animals in a trial of man before the animals:

> None are deceived by the words of an astrologer except tyrants and rebels among kings and oppressors among you.[52]

It appears that those who wrote the letters did not all have the same opinion on this matter, as evidenced by a comparison between the Animal Epistle and other letters, despite their emphasis on the necessity of intellectual harmony with their teachings.[53]

The importance of the Brethren of Purity's movement is not lim-

---

50   Epistles 42:4.
51   Ibid. 132:4.
52   Al-Rasa'il 350:2.
53   Ibid.

ited to their intellectual activity but also to their political and organizational work. They called for the necessity of cooperation between people and included an entire chapter on this topic in their letters, in which they called for a Mushtarak system, as they understood it according to the principles of brotherhood, cooperation, and the division of work according to specialization, ability, and social justice. They said:

> The individual cannot live alone except in hardship, because he needs various crafts, and no single person can master them all, as life is short and the crafts are many. Therefore, many people gather in every city or village to help each other. Divine wisdom and providence have necessitated that some engage in crafts, others in trade, some in construction, some in politics, some in the study and teaching of sciences, and others in serving the community and fulfilling their needs. They are like brothers from one father in one house, cooperating in their livelihood, each in a different way. As for what they agreed upon in terms of measures, weights, prices, and wages, it is wisdom and policy to encourage them to strive in their work and crafts and mutual aid, so that everyone earns a wage according to his effort and activity in work and crafts.[54]

We notice the similarity between this model of commonality based on brotherhood in kinship and what Caliph Abu Bakr said about Muslims being brothers who share equally in booty. However, there is a fundamental difference: the Brethren of Purity considered work as the basis for cooperation and wealth, not booty and war as in the early Islamic community. The Brethren of Purity called their brothers in several epistles to:

> "Abandon possessions except what suffices for hunger and to cover the nakedness."[55]

Naturally, their call for a society based on the division of labor would lead, if realized, to the establishment of a capitalist society based on the production and exchange of goods on a large scale. However, they called for human brotherhood in its broadest sense, saying:

> Some people have said: 'A true believer is not a true believer until he desires for his brother what he desires for himself.' This is not good enough. Rather, the wise and virtuous (may peace be upon him) said: 'A true believer is not a true believer until he desires for others what he desires for himself.' And this is the noblest of speech.[56]

And we do not know whether this paragraph was an attempt to

---

54   Epistles 99:1-100.
55   Epistles 254:4.
56   Epistles, 258:4.

expand the concept of the Quranic verse: "The believers are but brothers...,"[57] or just a presentation of a prophetic or philosophical discourse calling for brotherhood among all people. The Brethren of Purity affirmed their rejection of nationalistic boasting among nations and considered civilization to be the property of all people, regardless of their nationality or sect.[58]

The Brethren of Purity attempted, as their letters and narratives suggest, to organize a political revolution and overthrow the Caliphate system in the early fifth century AH. However, the plan was uncovered, and the Al-Qader Caliph, with the support of the Dailamites, was able to disperse their ranks. Al-Ma'arri expressed regret for their illusions of astrology and affirmed that the movement was in need for the sword, not just thought:

> Where is the group (of people) whose dwellings are demolished, and the whole living has settled in the tombs.
>
> A hope clings to the stars, so do not say our destiny is linked to a horoscope.
>
> We wished to acquire our goals with folly, it could not be obtained only by an unsheathing sword.

Despite the failure of the Brethren of Purity movement, it laid the foundation for a number of intellectual and revolutionary movements by establishing a strong political organization and linking political action to scientific education and simplifying human knowledge to make it accessible to the masses. One of the intellectual trends that emerged among the ranks of the Brothers of Purity was the school of Abu al-Ala al-Ma'arri.

AL-MA'ARRI AND THE MUSHTARAK THOUGHT

Al-Ma'arri represents the peak of communal thought in Islam. Although he joined the Brethren of Purity movement, he nevertheless distinguished himself from their utopianism with his materialistic and philosophical orientation and his call for the necessity of armed revolution to overthrow the Caliphate. However, he adopted from them the

---

57   Al-Hujurat: 10.

58   Epistles, 288:2.

strong political organization, the prudence towards rulers, the comprehensive global outlook, and the linking of scientific knowledge with daily revolutionary activity. In this respect, he went beyond the Brethren of Purity school in his view of the unity of animal life and the unity of the material world, seeing the need for harmony between humans and nature, not just internally—the nature of the human body—but also with the natural environment of humans. Hence, his call to respect the right of animals to life as long as they have come to this world involuntarily.

Al-Ma'arri took some of his ideas from Al-Mutanabbi, who left behind a significant school of thought, and one of his narrators was Al-Ma'arri's teacher in his youth. Al-Mutanabbi was an advocate of natural philosophy, which he learned in his early years in Kufa and later combined with communal ideas he acquired from the Qarmatians and the Bedouins near his birthplace. He passionately called for the overthrow of all kings and the use of the sword against tyrants. However, he retained an elitist racial attitude toward non-Arabs, as evidenced in his harsh poems against Kafour (the black ruler of Egypt). In this, Al-Ma'arri did not share his views, but contradicted him when he was still young, as shown in his poem *The Falling Spear*, whose opening line reads, "Blessed is the one who finds joy..." In response to Al-Mutanabbi, he said:

If a man knew his true worth,

He would not boast as a master over his servant.

Despite Al-Ma'arri's criticism of the Qarmatians for some of their esoteric beliefs and their enslavement of captives, he hinted on multiple occasions at his support for them and called for correcting their mistakes. He lamented their disbandment with the following lines:

The followers of Al-Hajari wished for victory,

Perhaps time would ease their sorrow.

Their group has become scattered,

Regret and sorrow cannot help them.

They said it would return one day,

and the rain would make the world bloom.

The verse was not cut off for a flaw,

But rather for correction and balance.

If you are given wealth, spend it generously,

For neither reverence nor hoarding keeps it.

He says that the Qarmatians were given a historical opportunity, but they squandered it due to a flaw in their formation. He likens them to a line of poetry that is fragmented by the weights of prosody, requiring correction and proper balance. It is as if Al-Ma'arri took upon himself this task. Al-Ma'arri believed that the problem was awakening the general populace, not merely isolated rebellion or individual leadership. He lamented the Qarmatians' failure to understand this issue, saying:

How many of the Al-Hajari and their likes have passed,

Whether they pleased or displeased the people.

Kings perish, and Egypt remains through their changes,

Egypt on the covenant and Al-Ahsa remains Al-Ahsa.

It is evident that he critiques the Ismaili movement, which established its state in Egypt, and believes that it fell into the same predicament as the Abbasids before them. In this, Al-Ma'arri refers to his political theory that the root of the problems in Islamic society was the existence of the state and the dominance of kings. Al-Ma'arri openly called for the abolition of the state and the establishment of a free society with no ruler and no ruled. However, as a materialist thinker (in the modern sense of the term), he understood that this was a distant goal that could only be achieved in an unknown time frame. But this did not prevent him from working towards that goal, no matter how distant it was. Al-Ma'arri believed that significant matters are made up of trivial parts, but if they were combined and continued, anything could be achieved. Therefore, he reproached the Brethren of Purity for their complacency, saying:

Whoever strives with determination in time benefits from it,

As he wishes, even to the extent of buying the full moon with the full moon.

He also expressed his revolutionary outlook, saying:

The arduous distance is traversed by short steps just as life is traversed by breaths.[59]

---

59   Al-Fusul wa al-Ghayat, p. 242.

Al-Ma'arri believed that the state is an institution based on injustice, and that it is a result of certain historical circumstances, and not justified by divine or natural reasons. It arose because some people prevailed over others due to the unequal conditions that the society experienced. He pointed to the existence of the Bedouins on the one hand and the cities on the other as a contributing factor to the prevalence of this domination. He said:

> There is no way (Sham) for the Sultan but to be shown
>
> The wealth of the Bedouins like ostriches on the run.
>
> And the nomads have sweet waters
>
> Like wine that is not lawful for any drinker.
>
> A king rules over people as if he were
>
> An angel tormenting the wicked rebel.
>
> With hands that kill every opponent,
>
> Striking with the cold iron sword.
>
> They said a just imam will rule us,
>
> Shooting our enemies with a powerful arrow.
>
> But the land is a dwelling of disputes and grudges,
>
> Never giving joy on any single day.
>
> If only it had an observer like Jupiter,
>
> Granting fortune, and a writer like Mercury.

The meaning of this passage is that the fate of the state and the king is towards disintegration and transformation into Bedouinism. Then the cycle starts again with the emergence of another king who kills dissenters with iron, and it ends just like the first. In his opinion, the state is based on domination and oppression, and therefore he ridicules those who hope for a just king who will repel their enemies, because the king and the ruler by nature lead to evil and animosity. Even if Al-Mushtari (Jupiter), who is known for justice and prosperity in the beliefs of astrologers, were in charge, he would end up like the kings who preceded him. All of this means that Al-Ma'arri did not accept the state and the division of people into rulers and ruled, and he expressed his opinion in many of his poems and sayings, including his statement:

> The leadership and the ruled, which are the root of malice, should not rule

or be leaders.

And he also said:

A foolish man wished for a kingdom,

Even if he had seized all the realms, it would not suffice him.

And the kingship is a solid mountain,

Which the vicissitudes of time establish and then uproot.

Al-Ma'arri believed that the foundation of human freedom lies not only in the abolition of the state but also in the communal ownership of property and cooperation in productive work. He viewed private ownership as contrary to nature, a phenomenon known to humanity due to the social decline brought about by civilization. In this regard, he considered humans to have fallen below the level of animals, stating that sharing is a natural law:

Among animals, there is sharing of land and air,

with Division will eventually be realized.

Kinship has not separated people

Whose father is Japheth and your father is Shem.

Al-Ma'arri observed that animals share in the wild, but ignorance and greed have led humans to enslave both whites and blacks and to kill Arabs and Romans, even though they are all children of one father—an allusion to Noah's three sons: Shem, the father of the Arabs, Ham, the father of Africans, and Japheth, the father of the Romans and Slavs. As a proponent of communalism, Al-Ma'arri openly stated:

If I or anyone else had as much as a fingertip's worth

Above the earth, I would consider the matter communal.

From this perspective, Al-Ma'arri believed that human work is the optimal source of life, while exploiting the labor of others, stealing their fruits of their work, and dominating and oppressing them is injustice and a decline in humanity. He expressed this in many of his poems, where he said, "Work and eat,"[60] forbidding the use of the sword as a means of earning a living. Therefore, Al-Ma'arri believed that the exis-

---

60   Al-Luzumiyyat 76:2.

tence of armies and the profession of swordsmanship symbolized social injustice. In this regard, he was influenced by the revolution of textile workers in Baghdad against the Caliphate's army when they were subjected to unjust taxes, so they rebelled and took refuge in the circular mosque. However, after a period of time, the Caliphate's spears were able to suppress them, so Al-Ma'arri said:

> When the spears of the spearmen drew near, the rods were raised, like spinning wheels and spindles,
>
> They called upon their Lord to destroy the swords and spears, and each has its end by God's power.

To emphasize this meaning, he also said:

> Seek sustenance by passing through the trees, not by the points of spears and swords.

And he also said:

> O you who wield the spear in order to consolidate the kingdom,
>
> It is better to use a digging tool or a hoe, than to use a spear.

Here, the "hoe" refers to the speed of work or a tool for digging the ground. Thus, the meaning is that work is better than carrying a weapon to consolidate the rule of tyrants.

In the poetry and writings of Al-Ma'arri, the idea of abolishing the state as an institution of oppression and exploitation is clearly evident. He developed an old idea that was opposed to the state, which was stated by many thinkers before him, and undoubtedly, its origins are derived from the memories of the *Jahiliya* (pre-Islam) society and the condemnation of the tyranny system. It has been mentioned that Al-Asamm was among the Mu'tazilites who denied the necessity of imamate [divinely appointed leadership] in Islam. This anti-state trend was developed by Islamic scholars such as Al-Biruni, and later on by Ibn Rushd, and its reflections were found in the writings of Ibn Khaldun.

Al-Biruni described some primitive societies to illustrate his idea of the origins of the state, noting that these societies viewed leadership with aversion. The person appointed to this role performed it unwillingly and, once his term ended, gave alms to the poor as if relieved of a heavy burden. Al-Biruni mentioned that they assigned leadership roles to some of their nobles in rotation, similar to assigning tasks like guarding or farming, and said:

> It is said about the inhabitants of a certain region at the farthest reaches of the Maghreb that the leadership rotates among their notables and trusted individuals for terms of three months. The person then voluntarily steps down at the end of his term, gives alms in gratitude, and returns to his family happily, as if freed from a shackle, and resumes his own affairs. This is because the essence of leadership and governance is to forsake comfort for the comfort of the governed, to ensure justice for the oppressed against their oppressors, to devise strategies for their defense in battles, and to divide the collected resources equitably among them as a wage, similar to what is collected for the town's guard or the caravan's protector, according to his role and rank, until his term ends...[61]

Al-Biruni's idea of leadership as a function that serves the community, rather than as a means of domination, reflected the new democratic trend that emerged during the decline of the caliphate and the rise of despotism. This concept, as we have seen, was mirrored in different forms in the writings of Al-Farabi, who advocated for the Virtuous City and collective leadership in Plato's *Republic*. Al-Biruni considered the Rashidun Caliphate an example of virtuous leadership free from tyranny. He denounced the transformation of the Islamic state into a hereditary monarchy under Muawiya's rule.[62]

The idea of abolishing the state and replacing it with a society-managed administration became a common topic among Islamic thinkers and historians. Ibn Khaldun mentioned this issue in his "Muqaddimah," where he stated:

> And what you hear about civil politics is not related to this type (i.e., sultanic politics). Instead, its meaning among the wise is what each member of that society should be in terms of their character and behavior so that they become self-sufficient and do not need rulers at all. They call the society where this is achieved the Virtuous City, and the laws observed in it are called civil politics. Their intention is not the politics imposed on society by general interests, as this is different from that. This Virtuous City, according to them, is rare and difficult to achieve; they speak of it as a hypothesis and a theoretical construct."[63]

---

61   Al-Jamahir fi Ma'rifat al-Jawahi, p. 30.

62   See Ibn Rushd's commentary on Plato's *Republic*—in English—as the original Arabic text is lost, pp. 223, 291.

63   Muqaddimah, p. 240.

From the above, we can see that Al-Ma'arri's call to abolish the state was not an isolated phenomenon in Islamic intellectual life but a developed expression of an old trend dating back to the pre-Islamic era. This idea was echoed by several thinkers and jurists and gained new content during the decline of the Abbasid Caliphate, the development of the capitalist economy, the flourishing of philosophical movements, and the emergence of popular revolutions. What distinguishes Al-Ma'arri's call from those of Al-Farabi and the Brethren of Purity is his understanding of the limitations of his era. He focused on educating the masses and organizing a circle of intellectuals around him. He expressed his ideas in a poetic style filled with enigmas but succeeded in conveying them to many generations despite the vicissitudes of time and the destruction of his works by the Crusaders when they occupied Ma'arrat al-Nu'man.

The highest goal Al-Ma'arri worked for, dedicated his life to, and forsook comfort and family life for, enduring much suffering, was to emphasize the idea of freedom, which he considered the most valuable thing in human life. He said: "Be free and settle wherever you wish, even in the heart of fire."[64]

---

64   Al-Fusul p. 282.

AL-MUSHTARAK AND THE MODERN SOCIALIST MOVEMENT

THE modern socialist movement emerged in response to two significant revolutions in Europe. The first was the Industrial Revolution, which brought forth modern industry, consolidated the global capitalist market, and unveiled the industrial working class. The second was the French Revolution, which established the democratic form of the modern bourgeois state, deepened national sentiment, and fostered divisions among European societies along national lines. The socialist movement traces its origins back to the publication of the *Communist Manifesto* in 1848, written by Marx and Engels. The history of the modern global communist movement, along with its accomplishments and setbacks, is intrinsically connected to the development of the modern socialist movement. To grasp its complexities, it is essential to comprehend the social and historical conditions in which it arose, particularly within the context of modern Western European societies.

1. The Nature of the State in European Capitalism

European capitalist societies differ fundamentally from Islamic societies, not only because European capitalism emerged in later historical conditions, but also because of the unique features of social and political formation in Western Europe. This region of the world relied on rain-fed agriculture, so there was no need for a central organization to regulate irrigation, allowing small population centers to be independent from each other. This explains why the family was the social and economic unit in these societies, where one family represented a complete economic unit as Marx said. This small economic formation allowed each agricultural family to be relatively independent of its peers, and individualism and nationalism were later manifested in European capitalist formation. In addition to this, the region was lagging behind the cultural development witnessed in Asia, the Mediterranean, and North and East Africa. European monarchies deteriorated significantly with the fall of the Roman Empire in Europe and its transfer to Constantinople. It is well known that what distinguished the European feudal system was the weakness of the central state and the actual political authority resting on feudal land ownership. Each feudal landholding formed a small duchy named after the capital of the 'state'—i.e., the king.

When European capitalism emerged, it appeared in the new commercial cities that grew with the expansion of world trade and commerce with Islamic countries. This explains the prosperity of Italian commercial cities with their trade with Egypt and Asian Islamic countries through Constantinople, and the growth of northern European trade through what was called 'the Rus'— that is, the inhabitants of Sweden and Norway who controlled Islamic trade through the Black Sea and then transported it to northern Europe via Russian rivers.

The formation of European commercial cities had significant political and social consequences that were reflected in the form of modern European capitalism. European capitalism was not able to control central state power except in very late stages—especially in the English Revolution of 1688 and the French Revolution of 1789. The state in which European capitalism grew was absolute monarchy, a despotic authority with feudal origins, but it sided with the commercial cities against the feudal noble authority, thus serving capitalist development. However, it later became a victim of this development when the bourgeoisie of the cities grew stronger and no longer needed the services of kings. Absolute monarchy became a major obstacle in the way of later capitalist development.

One of the consequences of capitalist development was a relative separation between capitalist ownership of means of production and the capitalist state. The state acted as a servant to the owners of factories, banks, and land, and did not play a direct role in the production process. This resulted in a relative distinction in European capitalist societies between the owners of means of production and the rulers. This does not mean that the state was not subject to the capitalist class, but rather that the relationship was more complex than its Islamic counterpart.

Al-Biruni[1] accurately expressed the nature of the Islamic state when he said, "Capital is the state," whereas in Western capitalism there was an indirect relationship between the state and wealth that allowed the European state to play relatively independent roles from classes during important periods in history. This was the case under the absolute monarchies in the seventeenth and eighteenth centuries and during the emergence of Bonapartist regimes that claimed to be revolutionary and served capitalism while pitting conflicting classes against each other.[2] The liberal form of the European capitalist state was the best political form that suited the development of free capitalism and free competition in the market. In this state, as Engels said, "wealth exercises its power indirectly and in the safest way."[3] This was confirmed by the *Communist Manifesto*: "The executive of the modern state is but a committee for managing the common affairs of the whole bourgeoisie."

Needless to say, this statement assumes the existence of capitalism outside of the state apparatus, where productive work and financial speculation are carried out, and the state in this economic model constitutes a management apparatus subordinate to a class that owns the means of production. This particular feature of European capitalism distinguishes it completely from capitalism in Islam, where the state-owned agricultural land, mills, and the largest industrial and commercial institutions in the country. This form of capitalism, as we have explained, led to the consolidation of individual despotism, which united all political, economic, and spiritual authorities in the hands of the Caliphate.

Therefore, a change in the ruling persons sometimes meant a change in the nature of the social formation, such as the deterioration towards military feudal relations or the substitution of a consumption pattern instead of focusing on production and commercial speculation. This is

---

1   **Ed. Note:** Abu Rayhan al-Biruni was a scholar, scientist, and polymath who was born in the year 973 CE in Khwarezm, which is now part of Uzbekistan. Al-Biruni made significant contributions to various fields, including mathematics, astronomy, geography, history, linguistics, anthropology, and pharmacology.

2   See Engels, *The Origin of the Family, Private Property, and the State*, International Publishers,1972 (English translation) p.227.

3   Ibid., p. 228.

evident even under one ruling family, such as the Abbasid and Umayyad dynasties[4] before them, when the rise of the Marwani family led to a shift towards capitalist economics.

In the Western European capitalist system, however, it was not a matter of the ruling persons. Governments may change while the class that owns the means of production remains the same, or it may even become stronger and its interests more concentrated as a result of replacing governors who do not align with its will and interests. The European bourgeoisie exercises its control through its wealth, extensive relationships, and influence over the governors. This control ensures the development of capitalism without relying on one dictator who creates whatever he wishes, sometimes without considering the interests of the class he represents or governs on behalf of. Lenin explained this particular feature of liberal bourgeois state when he said:

Another reason why the omnipotence of 'wealth' is more certain in a democratic republic is that it does not depend on defects in the political machinery or on the faulty political shell of capitalism. A democratic republic is the best possible political shell for capitalism, and, therefore, once capital has gained possession of this very best shell (through the Palchinskys, Chernovs, Tseretelis and Co.), it establishes its power so securely, so firmly, that no change of persons, institutions or parties in the bourgeois-democratic republic can shake it.[5]

This type of state is clearly more flexible and stable than a system based on the whims of a dictator or absolute monarch, and it includes the possibility of portraying it as a rule of the entire people because of the hidden ties that connect it to the owning class of the means of production. Therefore, such a liberal form is more capable of deceiving the masses and absorbing popular anger. Naturally, this situation represented free capitalism in its youth, but nowadays there is nothing left of imperialist monopolistic bourgeois liberalism except its appearances, as monopolistic state capitalism has developed in all advanced capitalist countries and the state has become a fundamental factor in the process of production and management of the socio-economic system. This ex-

---

4 **Ed. Note:** See Appendix I for dates.

5 Lenin, *The State and Revolution*, Progress Publishers, Moscow, 1918. Ch. 5, Section 3.

plains the growth of fascist trends in advanced capitalist countries and the enhancement of the role and size of the machinery of repression and espionage therein.

2. The Conditions for the Modern Socialist Revolution

The development of modern industry, the emergence of industrial working classes, the significant progress in human knowledge, and the domination over natural forces have provided and continue to provide, since the 18th century, a vision for organizing human society according to a new pattern free of exploiting humanity or nations. The new horizons opened up by modern historical development were the basis for the emergence of the modern socialist movement and its transformation from utopian dreams to a revolutionary social science. However, utopian socialism remained the dominant form of the socialist movement for a period of time. This movement was based on imagining small socialist communities on distant islands, and in other cases attempting to build such communities within the prevailing capitalist relations in society. Despite the deep criticism of capitalism presented by these utopian movements and their demonstration of the possibility of organizing society on new, exploitation-free foundations, all of their experiments failed and became an obstacle to the development of the revolutionary socialist movement among the masses of the working class. They called for moving away from political struggle and focused only on developing new forms of small socialist colonies, leaving the capitalist control of society intact.

Through criticizing these utopian movements, Marx and Engels developed the scientific theory of socialism, which saw the working class as the historical force relied upon in building a new society. Marx and Engels conducted extensive studies of modern philosophy and world history, introducing the materialist concept of history, analyzing the processes of capitalist production, and illustrating the mechanisms of capitalist exploitation as a new form of slavery based on the purchase of free labor. Marx and Engels concluded that the working class cannot build a socialist society without seizing political power, and thus political struggle is a necessary condition for the establishment of a scientific socialist movement. In the *Communist Manifesto*, Marx and Engels outlined the mission of the working class and their communist movement as follows:

> The immediate aim of the Communists is the same as that of all other proletarian parties: formation of the proletariat into a class, overthrow of the bourgeois supremacy, conquest of political power by the proletariat.

He also said, after a discussion of the content of the socialist movement:

> The first step in the revolution by the working class is to raise the proletariat to the position of ruling class to win the battle of democracy. The proletariat will use its political supremacy to wrest, by degree, all capital from the bourgeoisie, to centralize all instruments of production in the hands of the State, i.e., of the proletariat organized as the ruling class; and to increase the total productive forces as rapidly as possible.

It is clear that the modern socialist movement sees political revolution as the first and prerequisite condition for the establishment of a socialist society. In this respect, socialist revolution differs from the bourgeois revolution in Western Europe. The European bourgeoisie grew and developed within the feudal society of the free trade cities and the communes of the Middle Ages, and was able to exercise political power and military organization on the scale of the free cities for a long time, lasting for seven centuries in some regions. The major bourgeois revolutions in the Netherlands, Britain, France, and America were only the culmination of a long historical process, whose earliest beginnings date back to the tenth century or even earlier. Modern socialist revolution, on the other hand, had to initiate its own path, learning from its setbacks and from the experiences and lessons of history and human sciences. This means that its progress is often slow and subject to political setbacks, twists, and turns. All of this makes the socialist revolution a long and difficult historical task, full of setbacks and political retreats, and it is for this reason that it requires the necessary conditions to achieve genuine progress, which have been paved through a variety of experiences of victories, defeats, and historical twists. This is why Marx said:

> ...the proletarian revolutions, like those of the nineteenth century, constantly criticize themselves, constantly interrupt themselves in their own course, return to the apparently accomplished, in order to begin anew; they deride with cruel thoroughness the half-measures, weaknesses, and paltriness of their first

attempts, seem to throw down their opponents only so the latter may draw new strength from the earth and rise before them again more gigantic than ever, recoil constantly from the indefinite colossalness of their own goals—until a situation is created which makes all turning back impossible, and the conditions themselves call out:

Hic Rhodus, hic salta![6]

It is known that Marxism argues that socialism cannot be built on mere self-will, but must be established on specific material foundations and a scientific understanding of the historical and social development process. It was expected that the socialist revolution would triumph in Western Europe, as it was a developed capitalist region that contained organized working classes and possessed the material resources for building socialism. However, the historical path proved that the socialist revolution faced major obstacles in that region that was prepared for revolution, while the modern socialist movement found its main victories in the most backward regions in terms of industrial development, in Eastern Europe and Asia. This situation meant that socialism was built in backward societies, which made its path more complex and created new obstacles in its future course, especially in the face of the problem of overcoming bureaucracy, which must inevitably emerge in such circumstances and strive in various ways and methods to control the socialist state and direct it to its own class interests, as happened in most of the actual socialist countries. This is why the issue of the role of the state in the socialist revolution becomes the most important problem facing the working class in its struggle for freedom and for building a communist society.

3. What Can Replace the State?

This is a question that Marxism did not answer specifically until the Paris Commune of 1871. This is because modern socialism, as a science of revolution, did not present ready-made recipes for the nature of the

---

6 Marx, *The Eighteenth Brumaire of Louis Bonaparte*, International Publishers, (reprint 1963) 1852. [**Ed Note:** "Here is the rose, here dance!"—From Aesop's fable "The Swaggerer," a braggart claimed to have made a tremendous leap in Rhodes (which also means "rose" in Greek). When challenged, he was told, "Here is Rhodes, here leap!" Marx here paraphrased this as, "Here is the rose, here dance," a quote originally used by Hegel in the preface to his book *Outlines of the Philosophy of Right*, 1821.]

new political system in socialist society. Marxism learns from the popular movement and historical experience that people have in their struggle for liberation. As Lenin said, it is:

> A summing up of experience, illuminated by a profound philosophical conception of the world and a rich knowledge of history.[7]

The experience of the Paris Commune presented for the first time in history a modern, sophisticated form of the 'state' in socialist society. Here we use the term 'state' beyond the strict sense because the Commune is not exactly a 'state,' but rather a form of democratic political organization of socialist society, a form of the state on the path to extinction. Therefore, the experience of the Paris Commune remains the theoretical basis of Marxist teachings on the state in socialist society. Following the Paris Commune, Marx and Engels made the only amendment to the *Communist Manifesto*, which they found necessary to refer to in the introduction they wrote in 1872. They said:

> One thing especially was proved by the Commune, *viz.*, that "the working class cannot simply lay hold of the ready-made state machinery, and wield it for its own purposes."[8]

The impact of the Commune on the thinking of Marx and Engels was of great importance, to the extent that in 1875 they proposed the complete removal of the word 'state' from the programs of socialist parties, and its replacement with 'commune' and its equivalents in European languages. It is known that 'commune' means *Al-Mushtarak* in Arabic. This is because the 'state' is a tool of class oppression and a socialist movement that aims to liberate all workers and humanity from exploitation and injustice cannot aim to build a machine of repression and oppression. If it finds itself in need of a 'state,' it only needs it to suppress the overthrown classes, not for freedom, and this may lead socialist parties to remove all illusions about the true nature of the state among the masses of workers and to constantly strive to educate the masses about the class nature of the state and its repressive mission. From this perspective, Marx and Engels criticized the 'Gotha Program' announced by the German Social Democratic Party in the 1870s, which included among

---

7 Lenin, *The State and Revolution*, Progress Publishers, Moscow, 1918.

8 Marx & Engels, *Communist Manifesto*, preface, https://www.marxists.org/archive/marx/works/1848/communist-manifesto/preface.htm

its goals the slogan "the free people's state." Engels wrote in his criticism of that slogan:

> The free people's state has been transferred into the free state. Taken in its grammatical sense, a free state is one where the state is free in relation to its citizens, hence a state with a despotic government. The whole talk about the state should be dropped, especially since the Commune, which was no longer a state in the proper sense of the word. The 'people's state' has been thrown in our faces by the anarchists to the point of disgust, although already Marx's book against Proudhon and later the *Communist Manifesto* say plainly that with the introduction of the socialist order of society the state dissolves of itself [*sich auflost*] and disappears. As the state is only a transitional institution which is used in the struggle, in the revolution, to hold down one's adversaries by force, it is sheer nonsense to talk of a 'free people's state'; so long as the proletariat still needs the state, it does not need it in the interests of freedom but in order to hold down its adversaries, and as soon as it becomes possible to speak of freedom the state as such ceases to exist. We would therefore propose replacing the state everywhere by *Gemeinwesen* [*Al-Mushtarak*], a good old German word which can very well take the place of the French word commune.[9]

It is worth noting in this regard that Lenin, during the last few months before the socialist October Revolution, when preparing his book *The State and Revolution*, found it necessary to comment on Engels' letter mentioned above by saying:

> When reviewing our party's program, there is no doubt that Engels and Marx's advice should be taken into account, so that we can get closer to the truth, so that we can restore Marxism to its true form by cleaning it of distortions, and so that we can more accurately direct the struggle of the working class towards its liberation... Perhaps the difficulty lies not in finding the terminology. In German, there are two words for "community,"[*Al-Mushtarak*] and Engels chose the one that does not mean commonality individually but rather their combination, the system of communities. In Russian, there is no such word. Perhaps it is necessary to choose the French word "Commune," even though it creates some confusion.[10]

This position of being 'anti-state' was not new in Marxist writings, but became more apparent in light of the experience of the Paris Commune, after the model and political system of the socialist society became clear. Engels clarified this new view on the issue of the state in the

---

9   Engels to August Bebel In Zwickau, 1875, https://www.marxists.org/archive/marx/works/1875/letters/75_03_18.htm

10   Lenin, *The State and Revolution*, Progress Publishers, Moscow, 1918.

preface to the 1891 edition of Marx's work *The Civil War in France*, where he put forth a number of important ideas on the issue of the state, including his statement:

> The state, in even the best conditions, is a necessary evil, an evil inherited by the victorious working class to use against its class enemies... until the time comes when a generation raised under new, free social conditions can throw off the entire fetter of the state and consign it to the junk heap.[11]

From this, we see that Marxism adopted the *Al-Mushtarak* [commune] system as the optimal form of power for the working class in socialist society, and therefore represents the dictatorship of the proletariat, while at the same time reflecting the democratic, popular nature of this dictatorship. So what are the characteristics of the *Al-Mushtarak* system?

4. The Al-Mushtarak System According to the Experience of the Paris Commune

The *Al-Mushtarak* system emerged as a model for democratic socialism with the rise of the Paris Commune. However, its historical components and origins are derived from civic organizations that appeared in some European countries in the Middle Ages, despite significant differences from the Paris Commune of 1871. The latter was a socialist revolution in which the Commune appeared as a popular democratic form of the socialist political system, which in reality represents the dictatorship of the proletariat.

As for the medieval communes, they were civic communities and politico-military organizations that enabled developing European commercial cities to maintain their independence from the control of feudal nobles. They served as islands of bourgeois autonomy in a sea of surrounding feudal relations, and were referred to as "armed social associations with self-government" in the *Communist Manifesto*. This definition demonstrates the autonomy of these communities from the surrounding society. This self-reliance distinguishes them from the Paris Commune, which represented an armed political administrative unit in a unified system of communes that included the entire country.

---

11   Marx and Engels, *Selected Works*, Progress Publishers, 1969-1970.

One of the features of the Paris Commune was that it achieved a form of direct democracy that provided the masses with the opportunity to elect their representatives and withdraw them when necessary. These representatives formed the councils of the communes, which in turn delegated representatives to the higher political council. Thus, the commune became the smallest political-administrative unit with a self-reliant entity and centralized representation at the same time.

The communal system differs from the federal system in that the former consists of a single local authority in each commune, unlike the federal system, which assumes the existence of certain representatives or employees appointed by the central authority in addition to the local authority—such as governors and district officials, etc. In the communes, the elected councils form the only local authority, which represents the local population through elected delegates in the higher councils of political power in the provinces and through them in central bodies. Implementing the communal system, for example, in the conditions of Iraq, requires abolishing the positions of governors, district commissioners, and district managers and handing over all local powers to the elected local councils in each commune [*Mushtarak*]. Marx outlined the features of the communal system in his book *The Civil War in France*, which obviates the need to delve into the details of this system, and we will only refer to some of it in this document, as far as it relates to the research topic.

Marx, in his analysis of the emergence of the European bourgeois state, stated that its historical roots can be traced back to the Middle Ages. Its backbone consisted of the standing army, bureaucracy, judiciary, religion, and education. With the intensification of the conflict between capital and labor, "the state's authority took on more and more the form of a public force for oppressing labor, with its character as a class-state instrument."

The Paris Commune, which rose up in 1871, was the direct opposite of the French state under the Bonapartist Empire. Marx regarded the Commune as "a republic that was not only to remove the monarchical form of class rule, but class rule itself." Marx also pointed out the Commune's position on the standing army, stating that "the first decree issued by the Commune was the suppression of the standing army and the substitution for it of the armed people."[12] Lenin commented on this by saying, "[t]his demand is now raised in the programs of all parties calling themselves socialist."

Regarding the organizational structure of the Commune and the Communal system, Marx said:

> The Commune was formed of the municipal councilors, chosen by universal suffrage in the various wards of the town, responsible and revocable at any time. The majority of its members were naturally working men, or acknowledged representatives of the working class.... The police, which until then had been the instrument of the Government, was at once stripped of its political attributes, and turned into the responsible, and at all times revocable, agent of the Commune. So were the officials of all other branches of the administration. From the members of the Commune downwards, the public service had to be done at workmen's wages. The privileges and the representation allowances of the high dignitaries of state disappeared along with the high dignitaries themselves... Having once got rid of the standing army and the police, the instruments of physical force of the old government, the Commune proceeded at once to break the instrument of spiritual suppression, the power of the priests... The judicial functionaries lost that sham independence... they were thenceforward to be elective, responsible, and revocable.[13]

Marx distinguished between the communist system and the bourgeois parliamentary system, saying:

> The Commune was meant to be not a parliamentary body, but a working body, executing simultaneously legislative and executive power... Instead of deciding once in three or six years which member of the ruling class was to misrepresent the people in Parliament, universal suffrage was to serve the people, constituting the Commune in its own image. It was to be a working, not a parliamentary, body, executive and legislative at the same time... The Commune was to be a working, not a parliamentary, body, executive and legislative at the same time... The autonomy of the producers.[14]

Marx summarized the characteristics of the system of communes by saying that it was "the self-government of the producers."[15]

Regarding how social unity is achieved in this system, Marx answers

---

12 Cited in Lenin, *The State and Revolution*, Progress Publishers, Moscow, 1918.

13 Marx, *The Civil War in France,* accessible online at https://www.marxists.org/archive/marx/works/1871/civil-war-france/index.htm.

14 Ibid.

15 Ibid.

this question by saying:

> ...it was clearly stated in the National Organization's brief, which the Commune had no time to elaborate further, that the Commune was to... become the political form even of the smallest hamlet... the rural communes of every district were to administer their common affairs by an assembly of delegates in the central town, and these district assemblies were again to send deputies to the National Delegation in Paris.[16]

Regarding the functions of the central government in such a system, Marx said:

> The few but very important functions that would remain in the hands of the central government would not be abolished, and such an assertion was a deliberate forgery. Rather, they should be transferred to commune officials, that is, officials with specific and precise responsibilities...
>
> The unity of the nation would not be broken up, but on the contrary, it would be organized through communal construction. The unity of the nation would become a reality by destroying the authority of the state that claimed to embody that unity by gaining independence from the nation and dominating it. In reality, this state authority was nothing more than a parasitic growth on the body of the nation... The task was to cut off the oppressive apparatuses belonging to the old government authority, and to seize the legitimate functions from the authority that aspired to be above society and deliver them to responsible servants of the people.[17]

It is natural for the communal system to be subject to distortion and criticism from distorters and enemies. The famous distorter Bernstein attempted to attach the label of federalism to Marx's teachings and accused him of deviating from the principle of centralization. Lenin later responded to these accusations and forgeries, explaining the difference between the voluntary centralism advocated by Marxism and the "bourgeois military bureaucratic centralism." He said:

> People whose heads are stuffed with blind mythical faith in the state can see the destruction of the bourgeois state machine as the destruction of centralism. Bernstein cannot even conceive of the possibility of voluntary centralism, the voluntary unification of communes in crises, the voluntary blending of proletarian communes in the task of demolishing bourgeois sovereignty and the bourgeois state machine. Like all petty bourgeois-minded people, Bernstein imagines that centralism is something that can only be imposed from above, through the bureaucracies of officials and military cliques, as if Marx

---

16   Marx and Engels, *Selected Works*, Progress Publishers, 1969-1970.

17   Summary of Lenin, *The State and Revolution*, Progress Publishers, Moscow, 1918.

had predicted the possibility of distorting his views, meaning to indicate that accusing the commune of wanting to abolish national unity and central authority is deliberate forgery. Marx meant to use the term "organizing national unity" to oppose bourgeois military bureaucratic centralism with conscious proletarian centralism, democracy.[18]

Marx and Engels developed scientific socialist teachings about the state and the political organization of socialist society in light of the Paris Commune, calling for a socialist republic in the style of the Commune, rejecting the federal system in the Swiss style. Engels criticized the Erfurt Program adopted by the German Social Democratic Party in 1891, saying:

>...Thus a united republic, but not like the present French republic, which is an empire established without an emperor in 1798. From 1792 to 1798, each French province and municipality practised complete self-administration in the American style, and that should also be realized by us. As for how self-administration should be organized and how to dispense with bureaucracy, America and the first French Republic have shown and proven that to us... And such self-administration in provinces and municipalities is much freer organizations, for example, than the Swiss federation, where the jurisdiction is actually very independent of the Bund (i.e. the federal state as a whole), but is also independent of the judiciary and district. State governments appoint district directors and police directors, which is completely absent in English-speaking countries, and we must completely eradicate it in the future, like the Prussian conservatives and district directors.

Engels then proposed, in light of the above, that the German Social Democratic Party should strive to achieve:

>Complete self-administration at the provincial level... and at the level of jurisdiction or municipality through employees elected on the basis of universal suffrage, and the abolition of all local authorities and provincial authorities appointed by the state.[19]

From all of this, it is clear that socialism aims to achieve the broadest possible democracy in which the producing masses exercise their freedoms to practise governance, and then completely dispense with the state and all the violations of class agreements of organized repression and social violence against producers. This is the basis of the commune system, which we have translated into Arabic as the *Al-Mushtarak* sys-

---

18 Ibid.
19 Ibid., p. 450.

tem. We still need to examine how this system was applied in socialist revolutions that succeeded in the 20th century, especially the Russian and Chinese revolutions.

5. The Socialist October Revolution and the Mushtarak System

The Russian October Revolution of 1917 was the first successful socialist revolution and therefore gained special significance in the history of the modern socialist movement and in assessing what socialism has shown so far in terms of political and social organization forms for the liberation of labor. It must be said in advance that the historical importance of the October Revolution did not present a seriously complete new form for the socialist state, but rather aimed to achieve what the Paris Commune had accomplished. However, it was unable to achieve what it wanted and found itself forced to retract from the most important achievements of the Commune under the pressure of extremely complex and difficult circumstances. The results of these retractions later emerged in the context of the progress of socialist construction and the consolidation of the position of the Soviet Union internationally, and then in the entire course of the global socialist movement.

The commune system—the Mushtarak system—was truly the highest form of democratic political organization known to modern times, because socialism cannot be achieved except on the basis of the widest popular democracy. This fact, which emerged from the Paris Commune in 1871, was present before the eyes of the leaders of the Russian October Revolution years before the revolution, and the first Bolshevik generation grew and advanced on the heritage of the Commune and what it had provided in terms of lessons and experience for the socialist movement. This is clearly evident from Lenin's declaration upon his return from exile to Petrograd in early April 1917, where he said in his famous presentations: "We demand a state-commune."

Then Lenin clarified this demand in the article 'On the Dual Power' which was published two days later in the 'April Theses.' He pointed out the features of the proletarian power that appeared in a nascent form alongside the provisional government saying:

This power is of the same type as the Paris Commune of 1871. The basic features of this type are: 1- The source of power is not the law that has been previously discussed and approved by parliament, but rather the direct initiative from below, from the popular masses in their workplaces, and the direct "seizure," to use the popular expression. 2- The replacement of the police and the army, as two institutions separated from and in conflict with the people, by arming the people as a whole. Under this power, armed workers and peasants guard their own state system. 3- The officials and bureaucrats are also replaced by the direct power of the people, or at least they are subject to special surveillance and become officials not only elected but also subject to removal at the first demand from the people. Their position becomes that of mere functionaries, and they turn from a privileged class that earns high salaries in the bourgeois "winning positions" to workers of a "special armed force" who earn no more than the normal wages of skilled workers.

Here and only here lies the essence of the Paris Commune as a type of state...[20]

Lenin considered the Soviet councils as a similar model to the Commune, as they were direct instruments of power. He said about them:

A state of this model (the Paris Commune) was exactly what the Russian Revolution began to establish in 1905 and 1917—a republic of Soviets of Workers,' Soldiers,' and Peasants' Deputies and others, united in a Constituent Assembly of representatives of the people of all Russia, or in Soviet of Soviets, etc... This is what we have today, at present, arising spontaneously and in its own way, from the initiative of the masses of people, who are creating democracy in a natural way...

Lenin's call for a state modeled after the Commune faced many objections, as Russia was considered a very backward country that did not allow for such an advanced model of state to emerge. Lenin responded to these objections sarcastically, saying that they were just excuses of the feudalists who claimed that peasants were not ready for freedom!

These are the general outlines of the model of the state that the Bolsheviks sought to establish, according to the initiatives of the hard-working Russian masses and in the light of the experience of the Paris Commune, which as it turns out was based on the political model that emerged in the Commune.

---

20   Lenin, 'The Dual Power,' https://www.marxists.org/archive/lenin/works/1917/apr/09.htm.

6. The Practical Path of Socialist Democracy in the Soviet State

We have seen that Lenin and the Bolsheviks were determined to establish a democratic socialist state modeled after the Paris Commune. They had no ambiguity or hesitation about this issue and what it meant for building socialism in Russia. However, the nature of the state that emerged and solidified in the Soviet Union later on did not resemble the Paris Commune model except in name and appearance. The political system that existed since the 1930s relied more on the initiatives of central authority and party leadership than on the grassroots, the masses of producers, to the point where leaders were put in a sacred position that medieval priests could not dream of. We do not want to mention here examples that have become commonplace, such as the media idolization of leaders, their mummification, the suppression of the freedom of workers and peasants, and the grip of bureaucracies on the state. It is enough to point out the stagnation that affected the mass movement of this system that appeared under the name of socialism, against the wishes of its historical leaders. It is known that as soon as Stalin died, various accusations were piled up against his name, and the halos of individual veneration turned into insults and denunciations, in contrast to the fabricated highlighting of the roles of new officials who were preparing to take over the reins of power. And the verses of veneration were presented to anyone who was fortunate enough to rise to the seats of power. All of this was happening without any intervention from the popular masses, neither encouragement nor objection, as if it did not matter to them from near or far. All the changes that took place at the top of power and in the policy of the state began and ended in the state apparatus without the participation of the masses.

It is obvious that this raises various questions: What happened? Where is the Mushtarak system; the system of direct democratic socialism, from these situations that characterized the advanced stages of the Soviet state? And was it necessary for these phenomena to be associated with socialist construction, contrary to what socialist educators called for?

These questions require an honest confrontation. Avoiding them or attempting to find excuses means ultimately relinquishing the fate of the world socialist revolution and underestimating the interests of the labor movement. Without an honest and impartial confrontation of facts, it is impossible to discover the defects and then seek ways to ensure the progress of the socialist movement and the success of the just cause of the people. Our party has tried to answer these questions through several published documents and studies, so we see no need to repeat what we have previously presented regarding the reasons for the failure of the socialist revolution in the Soviet Union and other countries. Here, we point out two factors regarding the deviation of the socialist revolution in Russia: the objective conditions of the revolution on the one hand, and the development of Marxist theory regarding the state under socialism on the other hand. Concerning the first point, the Russian October Revolution did not only occur for internal reasons created by Russia's internal development, but also due to the global events that helped the revolution as the only way out of the Russian people's crisis. Without realizing the global and internal conditions under which the revolution took place, it is difficult to understand its subsequent course and the visible results today. Lenin describes the nature and reasons for the October Revolution in Russia despite its economic backwardness:

> It cannot be generally understood except by considering it as a link in the chain of socialist proletarian revolutions that are ignited by colonial war (i.e., World War I).[21]

It is clear that the October Revolution succeeded under exceptional circumstances that allowed the small Russian working class (which constituted only 13% of the total population before 1917) to lead the revolution and guide the Russian peasants against external intervention and famine and establish the Soviet Union as an advanced industrial world power. The dangerous role that revolutionary scientific theory can play in enabling a small culturally backward working class to overcome enemies of much greater class power was highlighted through the October Revolution. This was not only a testament to the courage of the Russian working class and the genius of its inspiring leaders, but also to the development of Marxist theory regarding socialist revolution and the strategy and tactics of armed uprisings. The Russian working class faced the task of taking political power and was intellectually and orga-

---

21   Lenin, *The State and Revolution*, Introduction, Progress Publishers, Moscow, 1918.

nizationally well-prepared to accomplish this historic task through its Marxist-Leninist party and long revolutionary struggles that lasted for about a quarter of a century before the October Revolution.

But this scientific superiority of Marxist theory was focused on the stages prior to the revolution; on analyzing capitalist relations and on revolutionary strategy and tactics. As for the construction of socialist society and the political organization of socialism, these were issues for which Marxism did not have the opportunity to study and develop a comprehensive theory. This is not a shortcoming of socialist educators, but a logical result of the nature of the socialist revolution. History had not witnessed a socialist society before the October Revolution, nor had the nature of the state and its role in such a society been scientifically revealed, and all that was available was a study of previous class societies. As for the Paris Commune, what it presented in this regard was only initial features of the democratic socialist system that did not have the opportunity to develop and mature.

For these reasons, the Russian working class had to pave a new path for humanity that was not yet known in its outlines, nor the nature of the obstacles that would be encountered in a very primitive manner. One of the reasons for its stumbling was this shortage of historical experience and the absence of historical data for the development of a scientific theory about the state under socialism.

It is known that Marxist-Leninism rejects utopian imaginations, as well as any attempt to impose ready-made and pre-prepared models on society. It sees the socialist revolution as a historical process carried out by the working class itself and its historical initiative. The role of scientific theory does not exceed summarizing historical experience and exploring the future outlines from tangible past and present facts. The attempt to depict utopian political or social models is not the task of scientific theory and does not conform to the requirements of historical development. What the scientific socialist movement seeks is to remove the constraints that limit the productive forces and the emergence of new labor relations based on the right of workers to the fruits of their labor, and to pave the way for the development of historical forces freely, rather than working to impose patterns of social relations inspired by the imaginations of isolated reformers and thinkers. However, rejecting the utopian approach does not mean, of course, leaving theoretical work and striving to develop intellectual weapons that enable the proletariat to pave its way to freedom from exploitation. It only means that the development of such weapons must take into account the reality of the historical movement, starting from the practical practice of class struggle and a correct understanding of the nature of the historical conditions in which the revolution takes place.

The deficiency in Marxist theory regarding the role of the state in socialist society is a natural result of the newness of the socialist experience. This is a fact that was apparent to the leaders of the Russian Revolution, as Lenin spent the last years of his life struggling against death, in an effort to develop a scientific theory to combat the growing bureaucracy and save the socialist revolution from drowning. However, the circumstances did not allow him to continue the battle, and this became the task of the second generation of Bolsheviks after Lenin's death.

As for what actually happened, the development of Marxist theory on the state did not occur during the second generation. Instead, there was a retreat from the important lessons of the Paris Commune, which was initially necessary and understandable, but later turned into a comprehensive intellectual approach that allowed the growing bureaucracy to seize control of the socialist state and distort its historical trajectory. We can observe the stages of this retreat and how it became the basis for organizing the Soviet state as follows.

Firstly, the Red Army instead of the Armed People

We have seen that the socialist parties' programs, in light of the Paris Commune experience, called for the permanent dissolution of the army and police and their replacement with an armed population. This was indeed achieved in the early days of the socialist Russian revolution, where armed workers and peasants replaced the tsarist army and revolted against government officers, merging with the revolutionary popular movement. However, this situation did not last long in the face of the great dangers that threatened the socialist revolution. The world war stopped, and the armies of imperialist states headed to strangle the Soviet republic, providing material and moral support to the tsarist generals and imposing a blockade on the young socialist state. Faced with external intervention, growing famine internally, and resistance from internal reactionaries, the Soviet state found itself facing serious dangers that it could not rely solely on the workers, peasants, and armed factions, nor could it be satisfied with the available defensive means. Thus, the socialist revolution had no choice but to retreat from the Commune program and form the Red Army. Lenin clearly identified the problem before the Eighth Congress of the Russian Communist Party, explaining the reasons that led to the organization of the permanent army:

> The nature of the problem we face is clear. If we do not defend the socialist republic with the force of arms, we will not be able to survive.[22]

Naturally, the reformation of the army meant the return of a large number of imperial officers saturated with hostility towards the people and the deification of brutal force. The Bolsheviks attempted to limit the danger of their decision by introducing a system of political commissars, intellectual education, raising class consciousness among soldiers, and involving revolutionary elements of workers and peasants in the army. These measures had their effect in facing the danger of the regular army turning into a force hostile to the revolution, but only for a time. When bureaucratic petrification appeared in the Soviet state and political power became concentrated in the hands of a few isolated from the masses, the army became the decisive force that tilted the balance in personal struggles for high-ranking positions of power. Thus, the Soviet army, since Stalin's death at the very least, became the actual force in the Soviet state, and the position of military leaders became the decisive factor in determining who would hold the highest positions of power in the party and the state. It is well known that Khrushchev, who inaugurated the era of military institutional control, was the first victim of it. This situation was then reflected in other countries bearing the name of socialism, in varying degrees of clarity.

There is no doubt that the origin of this problem dates back to the historical circumstances in which the first socialist revolution, the Russian October Revolution, triumphed, becoming the practical model for all subsequent socialist experiments. This problem is directly related to

---

22 'Report of the Central Committee of the Russian Communist Party (Bolsheviks) at the Eighth Party Congress,' *Selected Works,* International Publishers, New York, 1943, Vol. 8, p. 33..

the shortage of Marxist theory on the army and the state, as Lenin candidly pointed out when forming the Red Army, declaring to the eighth congress of the Bolshevik Party:

> The organization of the Red Army was a completely new matter, a matter that had never been addressed before even at the theoretical level.[23]

The danger of forming an army does not only stem from its use as a tool of oppression, but also because the army represents "the cornerstone of the state," as Marx and Engels stated (see the book *Revolution and Counter-Revolution in Germany*). From this perspective, the army constitutes the true state because it possesses the means to impose political decisions, by virtue of its monopoly on weapons. The meaning of forming a permanent army in a socialist society is the existence of two power structures: the armed apparatus, whose formal function is to protect the country from external aggression, and the political administration apparatus, which is supposed to exercise all the supreme authorities in the country. However, the truth is that actual power lies in the hands of those who hold the weapons. As long as the army maintains a certain degree of organizational independence, as required by military discipline, like all regular armies throughout history, it possesses the ability to exert its military force to impose any political decision that circumstances and internal balance of power enable it to enforce.

Military discipline is not subject to principled assessments or political discussions, but rather is a mechanical process that transfers the will of the military leadership to those under its command. The army's leadership may consist of revolutionary elements linked to the working class and subject to its political party, but this does not prevent changes in the nature of the army and military leadership, as long as the army's composition depends on its own lines that provide it with the ability to impose its will on the disarmed society. We say disarmed society because effective weapons become the responsibility of the army, and armed militias become unable to resist a unified regular army, as demonstrated by most of the events and coups in modern history.

Lenin had envisioned the creation of a defense apparatus, prior to the formation of the Red Army, consisting of all citizens between the ages of 15 and 65, with workers and employees being paid their full

---

23   Ibid.

wages during the short periods of military service. This system, if implemented, would have provided protection against internal reactionary conspiracies and repelled external aggression for a period of time, until the opportunity arose for a general mobilization. However, external intervention against the young Soviet Republic did not allow for the organization of such a popular defense system. When Lenin passed away, the Red Army became one of the "sacred" institutions that no longer aroused the reservations that had been expressed before. Therefore, this serious issue of great importance to the fate of the socialist revolution did not undergo a theoretical examination that matches its dangers and the political consequences it produced on the socialist system. It is beyond doubt that the issue of forming a regular army and securing popular defense against aggression are among the basic issues that every socialist revolution will face in the future. The more these issues are discussed and subjected to scientific debate before the revolution, and in the light of the great historical experiences accumulated since the October Revolution, the easier it will be to confront them in the future.

Secondly, Bureaucratic Administration Instead of the Soviet System

The second setback imposed on the October Revolution regarding the lessons of the Paris Commune was due to the same reasons for the restructuring of the regular army. However, the emergence of bureaucracy was a hidden process that was entrenched in the Soviet state apparatus, not due to a conscious decision by the revolution's leadership, and therefore its consequences were far-reaching and posed a deeper danger. It is known that it paved the way for the military institution's control later on. The Soviet system was akin to popular organizations that exercise direct political power and then voluntarily unite in one central council that represents the supreme authority of the socialist state. The backbone of the Soviets was made up of workers, peasants, and soldiers. However, these mass organizations found themselves having lost most of their 'politically aware' elements, which were not numerous in the first place, during resistance to external intervention and famine. The country's cultural influence had played a significant role in keeping the working class and poor peasants victims of ignorance and theological delusions. The percentage of literate people who could read and write until 1920 was not more than one in every three citizens, as Lenin indicated in his memoirs.[24] In such situations, it was not easy to compensate for the severe losses among conscious workers who fell in resistance to external aggression. It became necessary for the Soviet republic to recruit tsarist-era officials and bureaucrats in state institutions in exchange for high salaries and privileges that spoiled the spirit of volunteering and initiative in the ruling apparatus. It is not surprising that this social stratum, consisting of officials who were corrupted by the imperialist circles and trained in methods of flattery and evading responsibilities, found its golden opportunity in the ruins left by the war and famine to control sensitive state institutions and camouflage its effective anti-socialist role. However, the bureaucratic danger became clear in the second year of the revolution, which forced Lenin to shed light on it at the Eighth Congress of the Bolshevik Party. In his speech at the conference, he mentioned the proposed program of the new party, saying:

> Bureaucracy is attempting to regain some of its lost positions, taking advantage of the unsatisfactory level of public culture, and the tremendous efforts that have occupied the conscious section of urban workers beyond human capacity. Continuing the struggle against bureaucracy is an absolute necessity, and a matter that cannot be dispensed with in order to ensure the success of socialist development in the future.[25]

It seems from Lenin's later struggle against bureaucracy that his warnings were not heeded, and that the bureaucratic danger was wider and greater than it appeared on the surface. This explains the sharp language that Lenin took in his writings on this issue in his later years. He recorded in his memoirs while on his deathbed:

> ...the state apparatus we call ours is, in fact, still quite alien to us; it is a bourgeois and Tsarist hotchpotch and there has been no possibility of getting rid of it in the past five years without the help of other countries and because we have been "busy" most of the time with military engagements and the fight against famine.
>
> It is quite natural that in such circumstances the 'freedom to secede from the union' by which we justify ourselves will be a mere scrap of paper, unable to defend the non-Russians from the onslaught of that really Russian man, the

---

24   Lenin, *The Last Articles*, Progress Publishers, Moscow, 1924 (first publication), p. 24.

25   Lenin, *Complete Works*, Progress Publishers, Moscow.

Great-Russian chauvinist, in substance a rascal and a tyrant, such as the typical Russian bureaucrat is. There is no doubt that the infinitesimal percentage of Soviet and sovietized workers will drown in that tide of chauvinistic Great-Russian riff-raff like a fly in milk.[26]

Lenin confirmed on more than one occasion that the decisive factor in undermining the foundations of bureaucracy is educating the entire population to be able to manage their political and administrative affairs themselves without being subject to the exploitation of offices and rulers. However, the generation that took over the leadership of the Soviet state after Lenin's death did not realize the importance of this issue, and their main concern was directed towards economic development rather than building a new human being. Stalin's slogan was "technology decides everything," which reflects the need of the Soviet state to prepare for national defense against the Nazi threat that emerged in the mid-1930s. However, it also reflects the low awareness of the dangers of bureaucratic decay that had spread in the Soviet state. This bureaucratic stagnation was accompanied by the increasing role of the military establishment, especially in the aftermath of the appearance of Hitler's aggression against the Soviet Union. All of this was accompanied by the promotion of Russian nationalism to incite resistance against the Nazi invaders, gradually turning into a pattern of chauvinistic thought that justifies the annexation of spheres of influence and the exploitation of the wealth of colonial peoples and dependent countries. It was not strange, in light of all that, for the bureaucratic-military class to integrate and seize political power afterwards.

The decline of the socialist revolution extended beyond the Soviet Union to other socialist revolutions as well. However, notable distinctions exist between the events that unfolded in the Soviet Union and China. China's transformations followed a more comprehensive understanding of the Soviet Union's experiences and were preceded by a fierce ideological and political struggle between the two countries and their respective ruling parties.

China embarked on implementing a system, akin to the *Al-Mushtarak* system, which involved the establishment of communes in rural areas and initiated the 'Great Leap Forward' for economic devel-

---

26   Lenin, *Collected Works*, Progress Publishers, Moscow, vol. 36, p. 605.

opment. Internal conflicts within the ruling bodies intensified, leading to the emergence of the 'Cultural Revolution.' Despite the complexities and challenges associated with it, this popular movement, initiated by the masses and later led by Mao Zedong, significantly disrupted bureaucratic traditions and the entrenched leadership within the Communist Party. Its purpose was to prevent the stagnation of socialism, as witnessed in the Soviet Union.[27]

Despite the differences between China and the Soviet Union, as well as the distinct social circumstances in each country, the essence of what transpired in both aligns with the challenges encountered in constructing socialism across different nations. The absence of a scientific theory elucidating the role of the state in a socialist society is a recurring issue underscored throughout this document. Further contemplation on this specific point is warranted.

7. Marxism and the State

The topic of the state has held an important place in Marxist literature, where in addition to collecting the fundamental works of Marxist theory, specific authors have researched this topic, namely *The Origin of the Family, Private Property, and the State* written by Engels in his later years, relying on extensive notes left by Marx, and later Lenin's book *The State and Revolution*. As is known, Marxist research has focused on the origin of the state in history and its role in maintaining the social class system. However, Leninist Marxism paid attention to the topic of the role of the state in the future socialist society within the general theoretical limits allowed by scientific research. The Marxist theory on the state in the socialist society (the first stage of communism) is summarized in Marx's *Critique of the Gotha Program* where he said:

> Between capitalist and communist society lies the period of the revolutionary transformation of the one into the other. Corresponding to this is also a political transition period in which the state can be nothing but the revolutionary dictatorship of the proletariat.[28]

---

27 **Translators' Note:** Upon contemporary reflection, it is evident that China's subsequent remarkable economic progress, including the remarkable achievement of uplifting 800 million people out of poverty, would not have been possible without the Cultural Revolution.

28 Marx, *Critique of the Gotha Programme*, accessible online at https://www.marxists.org/ar-

In this precise definition of the role of the state in the transition from capitalism to communism, Marx refers to the transitional task of the state. Socialism cannot be built without the existence of the state for a certain historical stage, but this state has a transitional nature that is a revolutionary class dictatorship representing the working class.

Lenin pointed out that Marx's definition of the role of the state in the aforementioned socialist transition contains an important development of Marxist theory from what was previously proposed in the *Communist Manifesto* and other Marxist writings. The focus of the socialist movement before the Paris Commune was mainly on overthrowing the bourgeoisie and establishing power for the working class, achieving tasks that precede the building of a socialist society. However, Marx's writing in *Critique of the Gotha Programme* focuses on the issue of the transition from capitalism to communist society, which means future tasks for the state in the process of social transformation towards communism.

This new development in Marxist thought is of great importance, indicating an interest in the future of the communist movement and not stopping at past missions. The discourse now revolves, as Lenin pointed out, around a 'political transition phase' in which the state is a revolutionary dictatorship of the proletariat. History has proven the validity of this Marxist theory through several socialist revolutions, without a doubt. Without the dictatorship of the proletariat, the Soviet state would not have survived for days, not to mention years, and the same goes for the Chinese, Vietnamese, and other modern socialist revolutions. It is also known that the corruption of these revolutions did not arise from an external invasion or a counter-revolution from the deposed classes, but rather from internal deterioration within the apparatus of the proletarian power itself, confirming the transitional nature of the state in socialist society—meaning double transitional—meaning the possibility of transition to communism; to a society in which the state disappears. It also means the possibility of returning to capitalism through the state itself, due to bureaucratic decay. In fact, there is no historical dispute over the necessity of the dictatorship of the proletariat to transition to a communist society. Those who opposed Marx's argument in modern times were not motivated by a desire for the future of

chive/marx/works/1875/gotha/ch04.htm.

communism, but rather for the purposes of bargaining with imperialist bourgeoisie or misleading the working class and concealing bureaucratic control. It is known that those who called for the removal of the dictatorship of the proletariat from the programs of communist parties were the new leaders of the Communist Party of the Soviet Union, who took over the leadership of the Soviet state in the 1950s. Their goal was to conceal the new bureaucratic dictatorship internally and to facilitate bargaining with American imperialism abroad, and their claim was not associated with the "elimination of the necessity" of the dictatorship of the working class for any expansion of democratic freedoms for the Soviet people, but the opposite. As for those who called for the removal of the dictatorship of the proletariat from communist programs in Western Europe, they were hoping to gain the approval of their ruling bourgeoisie in the hope of immediate parliamentary gains. After their initial concession, as is well known, a series of other concessions followed, which in many cases led to the abandonment of Marxism-Leninism as a whole.

In summary, the theory of 'the political transition stage' and the necessity of the dictatorship of the proletariat in this stage for the transition to communism is a theory that has been fully proven by history and will remain a weapon for every socialist revolution in the future until the disappearance of classes and with it the disappearance of all states. However, this statement cannot include the second Marxist theory about the state under socialism, namely the theory of "the spontaneous withering away of the state." It has become clear that the tangible historical development of socialist revolutions in the 20th century has surpassed this latter theory, and it has turned into its opposite, becoming a weapon in the hands of the ruling bureaucracies in former socialist countries to seize the freedoms of the workers and corrupt the socialist revolution.

It must be said beforehand that the theory of the "spontaneous withering away" of the state was proposed in specific historical circumstances necessitated by the need to expose the anarchistic calls that had a wide influence within the socialist movement in the last century. The main efforts of anarchism were to call for the "abolition of the state" all at once without achieving the social revolution. The meaning of this call was to distance oneself from political work and the organization of the working class and to strive to seize state power from the bourgeoisie.

Therefore, it was incumbent upon the Marxist movement to engage in a broad intellectual struggle to refute anarchism and expose its influence among the working class, and to prepare the proletariat to engage in the political struggle for revolution. The danger of anarchist thought was great in the first stage of the Marxist movement, and the call to "abolish the state" was one of the slogans that hindered the consciousness of the working class at that time. As Engels mentioned in an article he wrote in 1850 in response to that slogan: "The abolition of the state, anarchy, has become the prevailing cry in Germany."[29]

Marx and Engels had to devote significant efforts in their early political lives to combat the anarchist tendencies among workers and young socialist organizations. It is known that anarchism emerged in Western Europe before Marxism did. Proudhon, the founder of this movement, published his major work *What is Property?* in 1840 before Marx and Engels began their activity. Marx was compelled to dedicate his first important theoretical work to respond to Proudhon and published his book *The Poverty of Philosophy* in 1848 as part of the theoretical struggle against anarchism and against petit bourgeois socialism. During the revolutions of 1848, anarchist thought spread more widely than before, so Marx and Engels wrote several articles to respond to the anarchist slogan of "abolishing the state." In a joint article to respond to this slogan, they wrote in 1850:

> For Communists, the abolition of the state can only be achieved as a necessary result of the abolition of classes—which, with their disappearance, automatically removes the need for organized force in the hands of one class for the suppression of others.[30]

As is known, the anarchists had significant influence in the Paris Commune of 1871, so it was necessary for Marx and Engels to continue their intellectual struggle against this petit bourgeois trend and to direct the working class towards political struggle for state power. The dispute between Marxism and anarchism in this regard was so critical that any tolerance or leniency towards it would lead to the loss of the entire working class cause. The issue was not just battles over the meanings of words and slogans, as Engels said:

---

29 Marx and Engels, *Collected Works*, 487:10.

30 Ibid., p. 333.

The dispute is essential: without a social revolution, the abolition of the state becomes nonsense. Abolishing capital is precisely the social revolution, which involves a change in the entire pattern of production.[31]

Marx and Engels returned to respond to anarchism even stronger than before, especially after the anarchists attempted to take control of the First International following the Paris Commune, chanting their usual slogan of "abolishing the state." Engels sarcastically commented on them, saying,

> The enemies of authority demand that the political state be abolished at one stroke, even before the social conditions that gave rise to the state have been destroyed.[32]

In 1873, Marx wrote a scathing critique of the anarchists and their call to avoid political struggle, saying,

> If the political struggle of the working class assumes revolutionary forms, and if the workers establish their revolutionary dictatorship in place of the dictatorship of the bourgeoisie, they commit a crime against the principles because, in order to satisfy their daily needs, which are of a brutal and revolting nature, they give the state a revolutionary appearance instead of abolishing it...![33]

It is clear from this intense ideological struggle between anarchism and Marxism that the danger of anarchism, which calls for the immediate abolition of the state and the avoidance of revolutionary political struggle, was a real and significant threat to the Marxist movement. Therefore, Marxist writings on the 'automatic withering away' of the state should be viewed in this context and within the atmosphere of the intense ideological struggle against widespread anarchism. In these circumstances, Engels wrote his famous work *Anti-Dühring*, in which he first introduced the theory of the "automatic withering away" of the state in the communist society. The paragraph in which this theory is mentioned deserves to be read in full so as not to be taken out of context. Engels said:

> The proletariat seizes from state power and turns the means of production into state property to begin with. But thereby it abolishes itself as the proletariat, abolishes all class distinctions and class antagonisms, and also abol-

---

31   From a letter dated 1/24/1872, *Selected Correspondence*, pp. 257-258.

32   As quoted in Lenin, *The State and Revolution*, p. 438.

33   Ibid., p. 435.

ishes the state as state. Society thus far, operating amid class antagonisms, needed the state, that is, an organization of the particular exploiting class, for the maintenance of its external conditions of production, and, therefore, especially, for the purpose of forcibly keeping the exploited class in the conditions of oppression determined by the given mode of production (slavery, serfdom or bondage, wage-labor). The state was the official representative of society as a whole, its concentration in a visible corporation. But it was this only insofar as it was the state of that class which itself represented, for its own time, society as a whole: in ancient times, the state of slave-owning citizens; in the Middle Ages, of the feudal nobility; in our own time, of the bourgeoisie. When at last it becomes the real representative of the whole of society, it renders itself unnecessary. As soon as there is no longer any social class to be held in subjection, as soon as class rule, and the individual struggle for existence based upon the present anarchy in production, with the collisions and excesses arising from this struggle, are removed, nothing more remains to be held in subjection—nothing necessitating a special coercive force, a state. The first act by which the state really comes forward as the representative of the whole of society—the taking possession of the means of production in the name of society—is also its last independent act as a state. State interference in social relations becomes, in one domain after another, superfluous, and then dies down of itself. The government of persons is replaced by the administration of things, and by the conduct of processes of production. The state is not 'abolished.' It withers away. This gives the measure of the value of the phrase 'a free people's state,' both as to its justifiable use for a long time from an agitational point of view, and as to its ultimate scientific insufficiency; and also, of the so-called anarchists' demand that the state be abolished overnight.[34]

It is clear from the text that it was written in response to the Anarchists and the advocates of the "Free People's State." There was no consideration for the possibility of the socialist state deviating, and the process of "disintegration" was considered completely automatic without the intervention of the governed; "it fades on its own." The truth is that this automatic nature has become a subject of questioning in light of more than half a century of socialist revolutions that encompassed about a third of the world. This formulation may be understood as denying or not taking into account the possibility of the state's survival for a period of time despite the absence of a need for it, because Engels refers in a number of other articles to this phenomenon: "When the socialist

---

[34] Engels, *Herr Eugen Dühring's Revolution in Science* [*Anti-Dühring*], pp.301-03, third German edition.

social system is established, the state dissolves itself and disappears."[35]

This spontaneous idea (in this sense) entered Marxist-Leninist thought before the October Revolution, affecting the development of socialism and the lack of sufficient vigilance against bureaucratic corruption. Lenin says:

> The expression 'the state withers away' is very well-chosen, for it indicates both the gradual and the spontaneous nature of the process. Only habit can, and undoubtedly will, have such an effect; for we see around us on millions of occasions how readily people become accustomed to observing the necessary rules of social intercourse when there is no exploitation, when there is nothing that arouses indignation, evokes protest and revolt, and creates the need for suppression.[36]

We will see that Lenin had revised these estimates in light of the emergence of the danger of bureaucratic decay in the Soviet state. The reality proved something else, which is that the state, even the socialist state, naturally tends to have complete control over society and does not want any habits other than submission and subservience. So how can the conditions and situation exist for the emergence of habits of self-management, habits of dispensing with the state and the people ruling themselves directly? Habits are assumed to be repeated over a long period of time until what was once conscious action becomes a spontaneous process that humans carry out almost unconsciously. And therefore, it is assumed that the people are accustomed to situations in which they do not need the state, long training in self-management, and the struggle against all attempts by the state to dominate society, which assumes socialist democratic freedoms that expand with the advancement of socialist construction and the consolidation of socialist foundations in society. And this assumes institutions for direct popular democracy that only a Mushtarak system can provide.

What can be said in this regard is that the theory of "automatic decay" was formulated in conditions where the dangers of bureaucratic decay of the socialist state had not yet become clear, and it was raised in conditions of growing anarchic calls to immediately abolish the state. If

---

35   From a letter from Engels to Bebel criticizing the Gotha program—cited in Lenin, *The State and Revolution*.

36   Lenin, *The State and Revolution*, Chapter 5, Section 3.

it had the "right to remain for some time for incitement" and responded to the ideas of petty bourgeoisie, it no longer matches the conditions of the retreat of modern socialist revolutions in an area that includes one-third of the earth's surface. A retreat that was not due to external aggression or an anti-old-class revolution, but due to the decay of the socialist state itself.

The theory of spontaneous decay, as presented, raises another issue as it assumes that social institutions will disappear automatically without external intervention, simply due to a lack of need for them. This argument may hold true for non-living processes or some limited cases of biological evolution, but human history has not witnessed a social institution based on privilege dissolve on its own without external intervention or without a struggle waged by opposing forces. The evidence for this is more than can be cited in this field. Let us take just one example: the need for capitalist relations ceased to exist since the beginning of the century, after capitalism entered the stage of imperialism, the age of world wars and the global economic crisis, at a time when technology had developed to high degrees that allowed the eradication of poverty, hunger, and disease from the face of the earth. However, this did not lead to the automatic dissolution of global capitalism or to its self-dissolution without resistance and revolutions by the people. Instead, it continues to strive with all the remaining energy it has to survive, even if it costs the destruction of humanity and the world's annihilation in a nuclear war. Furthermore, this also applies to the state in the socialist system, as it is an institution inherited from class societies that assumes the existence of privilege for rulers over the ruled. Therefore, it cannot simply hand over its 'keys' willingly and relinquish all its privileges automatically, without intense struggle and resistance.

And thus we see that the theory of the automatic withering away of the state in socialist society was a valid theory when it was proposed by the teachers of international socialism, in order to educate the working class on the importance of the dictatorship of the proletariat and to respond to the petty bourgeois anarchist tendencies calling for the "abolition of the state" and abandoning the political struggle against the bourgeoisie. However, time has surpassed it since the victory of the socialist revolutions in the Soviet Union, China, and other socialist countries, and since the emergence of the danger of the new bureaucratic class formation and the deviation of socialist revolutions from their correct path, resulting in the corruption of socialism and its transformation into monopolistic state capitalism with 'socialist' appearances.

The theory of the automatic withering away of the state is no longer in line with the historical experience accumulated through the rich and vast development of socialist revolutions in the twentieth century, after the anarchist movement was defeated and no longer poses a threat. Lenin was well aware of this fact in the last years of his life when he began to clearly perceive the danger of bureaucratic degeneration. He wrote at the beginning of 1923: "It must be acknowledged that there has been a substantial modification of our general view of socialism."[37]

And this modification that Lenin referred to is the transformation of tasks from political struggle against the bourgeoisie and preparation for the socialist revolution to the process of educating the masses and preparing the new socialist human who is capable of governing himself without the need for repression and terrorism that the state imposes. We have previously mentioned Lenin's criticism of the state apparatus during the October Revolution era, which he called a "bourgeois-Czarist mixture." Let us now emphasize the role that workers' unions and their professional organizations can play in protecting the socialist revolution from the state, even from the socialist state itself! He said: "We must use these organizations to protect workers from their own state..."[38]

It is clear, therefore, that the currency of the transition towards communism is not achieved in a spontaneous and natural way, without struggle from below, by the popular masses supported and directed by the vanguard of the working class. However, criticism of "spontaneity" is implicitly present in Engels' writings when he said: "Even in the best cases, the state is an evil inherited by the victorious proletariat in the struggle for class control..."[39]

Engels clearly pointed to the possibility of bourgeois reaction after the socialist revolution, stating in a commentary on the experience of the

---

[37] From the article 'On Cooperation,' *Collected Works*, vol. 33, p. 232.

[38] Marx and Engels, *Complete Works*, 25:23.

[39] From Engels' Introduction to Marx's book, *The Civil War in France*, 1891.

Paris Commune:

> From the outset the Commune was compelled to recognize that the working class, once come to power, could not manage with the old state machine; that in order not to lose again its only just conquered supremacy, this working class must, on the one hand, do away with all the old repressive machinery previously used against it itself,and, on the other, safeguard itself against its own deputies and officials, by declaring them all, without exception, subject to recall at any moment.

It is clear from this that the victorious working class must "protect itself from its own deputies and officials." Doesn't this mean that socialism does not rule out the struggle against the socialist state? It is now very clear that the theory of "spontaneous decay" was put forward in conditions of struggle against chaos as an alternative to the slogan of "immediate abolition of the state." However, in the current situation, continuing to cling to this theory will have a negative impact in the context of the victory of the socialist revolution and the emergence of the danger of bureaucratic degeneration. In these circumstances, it becomes necessary to overcome it and present a realistic analysis of the role of the state in socialist society, taking into account the necessity of mass struggle as a counterforce against bureaucratic degeneration and ensuring a greater transition towards communism. If this is the case, then it is necessary to consider the nature of the class state and the possibility of bourgeois reaction arising from within the socialist state itself; from within the dictatorship of the proletariat's apparatus.

And What Can We Conclude From all This?

FIRSTLY: The state is a tool of oppression used by the ruling class in society to maintain their hegemony and the class-based conditions of production. This applies to the state under feudalism, capitalism, and all class-based societies, as well as under socialism. There is no ambiguity in Marxist teachings on this issue or on the fundamental contradiction between the state and freedom. Engels criticized the slogan "free people's state" advocated by the German Social Democratic Party in the 1970s, saying, "Talking about a free popular state is just nonsense: as long as the proletariat needs the state, it does not need it for freedom but for suppressing its enemies, and when it is possible to talk about freedom, the state disappears. Therefore, we propose to replace the word 'state' with the word 'commune' everywhere."[40]

SECONDLY: The state, as a remnant of class-based societies, is a social institution based on privileges for the governed, and therefore it cannot be imagined abolishing itself automatically; "it dissolves itself" without a struggle by the governed in a socialist society. Thus, the possibility of a bourgeois relapse in a bureaucratic and rotten form remains as long as the socialist state exists.

THIRDLY: The state in general, and the socialist state as a social entity, has the ability to survive even after the conditions that brought it into existence have disappeared. This is because as a living social entity, it possesses the highest authorities in society and is capable of creating artificial reasons and factors to sustain its existence. In fact, whenever this entity loses its real justifications for existence, it tries to flood society with corruption and sabotage to create conditions that allow it to survive. It is capable of seeking artificial justifications, either by inciting external wars and spreading chauvinism and imperial expansion or by plunging society into deep internal conflicts. Our history provides an example of this. The Abbasid state lost its justifications for existence after the end of its golden age, but it continued to exist for a long time through artificial means that ultimately led to the destruction of both the civil society and the state. Class struggle does not always require one class to triumph over another; in some cases, it leads to the mutual destruction of all classes, as the *Communist Manifesto* pointed out.

FOURTHLY: The awareness of the working class, which has triumphed over the dangers of bureaucratic corruption, constitutes an important weapon that deepens the working class's resistance to any deviation that appears in the socialist state. Therefore, intellectual awareness of the nature of the class state is one of the guarantees against bureaucratic deviation in the socialist revolution. However, intellectual awareness alone is not sufficient to ward off bureaucratic forces that must inevitably form and grow in the institutions of the socialist state. This bureaucracy possesses the power of the state, meaning the power of the organized society within the state, and it is in a position to overcome the resistance of the working class and the popular masses under its rule,

---

40   Lenin, *The State and Revolution*, p. 440.

unless democratic and popular institutions are established to counteract its bureaucratic deviation and enable the masses to decisively overcome it. THIS IS PRECISELY THE TASK OF THE AL-MUSHTARAK SYSTEM.

AL-MUSHTARAK AS AN ESSENTIAL COMPONENT OF DEMOCRATIC SOCIALISM

AL-MUSHTARAK asserts that the specific form of the political system that will emerge from the Iraqi revolution cannot be predicted in advance, as this form is determined by the course of mass struggle through historical popular initiatives. It is not the task of the forces of change to come up with imaginary forms of political organization for the future society, but to develop what is creative in the popular initiatives to be the nucleus and foundation of the new system. The goal is not to invent a political system and try to impose it on the Iraqi society forcibly, but rather its task is to explore our people's historical experiences and draw scientific lessons from them.

Al-Mushtarak has not been proposed as a pattern of political organization imposed forcibly on our people, and it does not allow itself to impose anything on the popular masses. Rather, it presents a formula for the democratic socialist system inspired by the history of our people in line with the practical experience of modern socialist revolutions, particularly the experience of the Soviets established by the Bolsheviks at the dawn of their revolution. Moreover, when the authors of the *Mushtarak* propose the task of realizing the '*Mushtarak* republic,' they do not mean by that a rigid form of the socialist political system. Instead, they present broad general lines that help our people, as they approach the revolution, to find its path towards freedom through the rubble of previous centuries, amidst the misleading calls launched and being launched by the forces of deception and sabotage. This is in addition to the efforts of global imperialism and local reactionaries to keep our people enslaved and unable to secure their democratic rights and liberate their land and national wealth.

The basis of the *Al-Mushtarak* system is direct popular democracy that must be organized in effective political institutions in order to protect the rights of the people, train them in self-management, and provide them with the means to resist reactionary and imperialist pressures. The *Al-Mushtarak* system assumes the establishment of political and administrative units in geographically or nationally linked areas that do not exceed the ability of the people to manage directly. Each of these political-administrative units constitutes a single Mushtarak that includes at least a relatively large city and its surrounding villages and countryside. The geographical area of a particular Mushtarak is determined by direct consultation between the people and their elected representatives, and according to the economic and political considerations of the state as a whole. One Mushtarak can include a 'province' or 'district' from the previous administrative divisions in Iraq, or what may emerge from new divisions that may appear during the revolution according to the needs of the country. The main city of a Mushtarak is the local political and administrative center from which all Mushtarak's activities are managed, and it is linked to villages, countryside, and small towns. All local education and administrative institutions are affiliated with the Mushtarak, which oversees the local militias and military units formed by the people.

The affairs of the Mushtarak are managed by a council of elected representatives from the popular masses in the relevant area, both men and women, who are subject to the majority of voters who have the right to remove them and elect others at any time they wish. The council of the popular representatives holds all administrative positions relevant to the state, such as governors, prefects, district managers, and others. The police and popular militias in the Mushtarak are subject to the council of popular representatives and follow its orders.

The central bodies of the Mushtarak are composed of the Supreme Council of the Mushtarak, which is formed by representatives of the local Mushtaraks appointed directly through free and fair elections by the popular masses of each Mushtarak. The Supreme Council of the Mushtarak has the authority to elect state officials, legislate general laws for the country, approve economic and educational programs, and adopt the state's general policy.

The presidency of the state, the Supreme Council of the Mushtaraks, and all the higher central bodies of the state are rotated to ensure the maximum possible participation in the presidency of the higher bodies of the state and to remove any mythical authority of power. In order to protect the citizens' freedoms and prevent the rulers from dominating the people, an independent national high authority is formed, composed of popular figures with a prestigious position, which is responsible for considering citizens' complaints about the officials' encroachment on the people's rights. This authority enjoys political and legal immunity that protects it from state violations.

As for how the Mushtaraks are interconnected and how the national unity of the Mushtarak is maintained, this is a matter that we have previously discussed according to the experience of the Paris Commune and the political organizations of the ancient Islamic Mushtaraks in Kufa and Basra. In order to prevent the leading political parties from succumbing to corruption, bureaucracy, and integration with the ruling state apparatus, their entity must be based on democracy, and their membership and leadership must be subject to the people's supervision through popular oversight of their work and the nomination of their members. As it completely prohibits the association of party membership with any special economic or social privileges, the status of party members and their cadres should be the same as that of the entire people in terms of salary, housing, and all aspects of social life.

These are the general guidelines for the *Mushtarak* system. As for specific areas such as national defense, citizens' freedoms, and others, they require more precise determination because of their direct relationship with the lives of the masses and because they have become better known and more comprehensive in light of their historical experience. Therefore, they need to be addressed in more detail.

Firstly, Disbanding the Army and Replacing it with Armed People[1]

As Marx and Engels asserted, the first imperative of any successful revolution is to dismantle the old army and establish a new one. Lenin encapsulated this task in defining the socialist revolution, and indeed, any

---

1   Ed. Note: This following sections have been slightly updated to consider the US occupation of Iraq in 2003.

triumphant revolution.[2]

Without a doubt, this will be the primary undertaking of the new Iraqi revolution. To ensure stability for a democratic system that aspires to build socialism and progress towards a classless society, the disbanding of the government army, which was reconstructed under American occupation, is indispensable.

It is widely known that the existing Iraqi government army traces its origins back to the army established during British colonization following the 1920 revolution. It was crafted under the guidance of figures like Nuri al-Said, Ja'far al-Askari, and others associated with colonialism. Over time, the Iraqi army transformed into a repressive tool utilized to crush people's uprisings. Subsequently, it became an instrument in the hands of opportunistic adventurers and dictators to impose their authority.

The defeat of the newly formed Iraqi army by the caricatured entity of ISIS in 2014, an army established during the American occupation in 2003, and the emergence of the Popular Mobilization Forces, which thwarted the occupation's scheme and defeated ISIS, illuminate the path for the Iraqi people to defend themselves autonomously. This reveals the potential powers of the armed people and aligns with the insights provided by the Mushtarak study of 1983.

Incorporating patriotic elements within the government army does not alter its reactionary nature or its antagonism towards the Iraqi people's aspirations for national liberation, democracy, and social progress. These patriotic elements joined the army and preserved their lives not out of genuine patriotism, but rather because they were not targeted by the ruling reactionaries. Their political identity and connection to the people's yearning for freedom are severed in a critical moment, likely leading to a disassociation from the army and, perhaps, from life itself. Hence, these patriotic elements within the government army remain in military service as part of the establishment, executing military orders. Naturally, this does not imply neglecting the role of patriotic elements within the army in the broader revolutionary struggle. These elements prove significant during crucial junctures and when the popular revolu-

---

[2] Lenin, *Complete Works*, 284:28.

tion reaches its maturity. The same considerations apply to the leaders of the government army, comprising soldiers and officers who are essentially the defiant sons of the oppressed people. Once a soldier joins the government army, they become a blind instrument, their personal dignity violated, subjected to various forms of humiliation, serving as a voiceless tool directed by the military establishment for its own purposes. Nevertheless, the soldier remains the son of the people, often originating from the ranks of workers and peasants, and is expected to be influenced by the circumstances of the popular movement.

Therefore, advocating for the dissolution of the government army does not imply negating the role of patriotic soldiers and officers in establishing national defense agencies in the aftermath of the popular revolution's victory and the dismantlement of the government army.

What Replaces the Government Army?

The experiences of modern revolutions confirm the ability of the armed people to maintain their revolutionary gains. The armed people do not just mean a heterogeneous mixture of armed individuals, but rather that the duty of national defense, i.e. military service, is a duty of all members of society who are capable of bearing arms according to a system of continuous training and short-term service for a few days each month or each year, and a system of rapid mobilization in times of emergency. Such a system for national defense has become within reach of revolutionary systems, thanks to the facilitation of modern science and technology for the use of weapons and the simplification of the task of national defense. In the past, armies relied on cavalry and high skill in the use of hand weapons and primitive war tools. With the development of defense methods against modern armor and aerial weapons, the tasks of national defense have become accessible to all learners who can be trained for short periods of time to master the use of modern defense tools based primarily on scientific knowledge rather than manual skills and long training. Naturally, a national defense system based on the armed people is not suitable for expansionist wars and the occupation of other countries, and it is self-evident that 'socialism' that wants military expansion at the expense of other peoples is not socialism. Imperialist expansion is not what our people aspire to and is not what is meant by the Mushtarak system. However, if the task intended by the system of armed people is national defense, repelling foreign invaders, and suppressing reactionary rebellions, it ensures higher efficiency and lower cost to protect national independence and the gains of the masses.

There is no doubt that a defense system based on an armed population is an integral part of the general political-social system of democratic socialism. This system assumes the spread of scientific education throughout society, which may mean making higher education mandatory for all citizens in the circumstances of Iraq, given the small number of the country's population and the vast national resources available that require high productivity. In such advanced cultural levels of society, national defense requirements can be easily secured by introducing military education in high schools and universities as a basic subject in education.

The system of armed population assumes the existence of a permanent centralized structure for national defense as long as external dangers persist. The mission of this military structure is to prepare military training and planning, provide a nucleus of the popular defense apparatus, and mobilize all defensive capabilities of the population in the shortest possible time in times of emergency. Such a system has been implemented for years in some capitalist countries such as Switzerland, which planned its defense system based on continuous training and full readiness for war, and the ability to recruit half a million fighters within twenty-four hours. It is natural that the level of technological development in these countries allows for such a system, which has played a role in protecting them from foreign aggression for centuries.

This does not mean that such a system can be implemented all at once in the current conditions of Iraqi society, but it is possible to secure a defense system based on an armed population within the current capabilities of the Iraqi people, which ensures the successful defense against hostile attempts and secures the transition of socialist society towards full freedom and cuts off the path of bureaucratic-military corruption.

SECONDLY, DEMOCRATIC FREEDOMS

Democratic freedoms for the popular masses constitute the complete basis of the Mushtarak system. This system, as a form of direct popular power, cannot exist without the popular masses enjoying wide political freedoms in party and professional organization, expression of opinion, publication, and their right to access information on political developments and knowledge of what is happening in the state and the world.

Freedom of thought, publication, and the press constitute a fundamental cornerstone of any democratic system. A popular political system like the *Mushtarak* system cannot be imagined without the availability of wider democratic freedoms in order for the traditions of popular democratic governance to emerge and take root, and for the masses to learn the art of politics through their own experiences, through trial and error, criticism, and self-criticism, in order to resist attempts by bureaucracy to make the people ignorant and to spread the myth of the superiority of rulers over the governed.

The goal pursued by the communist system is to achieve complete freedom within a social system free from classes and the state, a communist society. Such an advanced society assumes a high level of human consciousness and the establishment of traditions of self-management of human communities without the presence of oppressive superstructures. These traditions cannot exist, become established, or gain comprehensive social respect without long-term practice by the popular masses of wide democratic freedoms and their realization of the value of freedom in practical application. It goes without saying that creatures born and raised in cages do not know the taste of freedom, and this truism applies to animals as much as it does to ignorant humans. Indeed, relations of slavery persisted in history for long periods even after the power of slaveholders had vanished. Nevertheless, some slaves continued to look upon their former masters with submission and refused any idea of exercising their human freedom. Those who are accustomed to humiliation and submission, and in whom habits of blind obedience to brutal force are deeply ingrained, cannot acquire in a single moment the proud and free spirit of a Bedouin, ready to die without hesitation in the face of humiliation and degradation.

Therefore, democratic freedoms in the communist system do not constitute mere gains provided by socialism to the popular masses, they are essential components of socialism. Without them we have a modern system of oppression regardless of what it calls itself, its names and attributes, and what it claims for itself in terms of features and objectives.

It is understood that an advanced political system such as the *Al-Mushtarak* system cannot emerge in a complete form without any shortcomings at once, but rather it must go through a long period of development and growth, interspersed with various obstacles, setbacks, and varying degrees of class struggles. It is also impossible to imagine a situation where global imperialism and deposed reactionaries leave the new system to live and develop peacefully. It is inevitable that the resistance of the deposed classes will intensify and persist in regaining their lost paradise, either through open resistance or through gradual espionage and corruption.

The reactionary forces, often with support from imperialist circles, aim to undermine the new revolutionary system by employing various tactics, including sabotage. They may try to pressure the system to limit democratic freedoms enjoyed by the masses, creating conditions that justify suppression. As a result, the revolutionary system is at risk of weakening its foundational principles. It is anticipated that local reactionaries and imperialist groups will utilize their media resources and intricate networks to sabotage the revolutionary system.

Such dangers will remain major problems facing every socialist revolution, and it is not appropriate to underestimate the capabilities of global capitalism and surrender to the deposed reactionaries.

However, the *Al-Mushtarak* system has effective weapons in the face of these dangers and reactionary conspiracies. The popular masses are attached to their revolutionary gains and are motivated to protect these democratic gains. Political awareness can also play an important role in mobilizing the masses against counter-revolutionary attempts. As much as the *Mushtarak* system represents the will of the masses, it is able to respond to attempts at deception and sabotage while protecting the democratic freedoms of the masses. It is also important to confront arms with arms. In such circumstances, the revolutionary system may not be forced to restrict democratic freedoms, but rather expand them as socialist construction advances and the consciousness of the masses deepens and strengthens the *Mushtarak* system. The revolutionary system must be careful not to use state power to confront all reactionary criticism, where the state becomes an alternative to the masses, thereby disabling popular initiative. This is because repressive methods serve reactionary governments and exploiting classes, but they may lead to undermining socialism by dominating repressive agencies and disabling popular initiative. We must remember that the ultimate goal of the modern socialist movement, as Lenin said, is "abolishing the state, i.e., all organized and systematic violence, all use of violence against people in general."[3]

THIRDLY, THE NATIONAL ECONOMY IN THE AL-MUSHTARAK SYSTEM

The *Al-Mushtarak* system assumes the establishment of a socialist revolution that ensures workers receive the full benefits of their labor, either through fair wages or access to social services. It emphasizes that socialism in the Iraqi context would not primarily entail confiscating the properties of the owning classes or nationalizing national wealth. This is because the Iraqi economy operated under a system of state bureaucratic capitalism during Ba'thist rule, where a significant portion of private sector wealth was already seized. Instead, the focus of the socialist revolution would be primarily on dismantling fascist institutions and establishing a system of popular democracy.

Following the US occupation of Iraq in 2003, there have been changes in ownership dynamics, with a shift towards the dismantling of state institutions and the promotion of neoliberalism. This shift is documented in Fouad Al-Amir's study on the rise of capitalist neoliberalism in Iraq.[4] Furthermore, attempts have been made to circumvent the nationalization of oil.

Regarding the private national industrial sector, the *Al-Mushtarak* system does not aim to seize or weaken it after it has already undergone liquidation, confiscation, and sabotage by successive governments. Instead, it is in the interest of socialist construction in Iraq to support the private industrial sector, allowing it to contribute its technical expertise to the development of the national industry, particularly in areas such as light industries and high-quality consumer goods. These measures

---

3   Lenin, *Collected Works*, 1971, Progress Publishers, Moscow, Vol. 25.

4   Fouad Kassim Al-Amir, *New Liberal Capitalism*, Alghad publishers, Baghdad June 2019.

would not undermine socialist production but could foster competition to meet the people's needs at the lowest possible cost and provide tangible indicators of the efficiency of the state's economic institutions. The Soviet state employed a similar system during Lenin's leadership without compromising its socialist nature. Furthermore, the Iraqi national bourgeoisie is more advanced compared to the Russian bourgeoisie of that time. Given the dominance of the state sector in Iraq's national economy, involving the private national sector in economic development for a certain period can be both feasible and beneficial. Such participation serves as a means to direct capitalist development in a transparent manner that can be monitored by the popular masses, thus posing less risk than the growth of black-market capitalism and its negative impact on the governance system and political stability.

The *Al-Mushtarak* system should prioritize directing substantial national efforts towards revitalizing Iraqi agriculture, which has suffered from deterioration and destruction caused initially by the Ba'th regime and later exacerbated by the US occupation in 2003. This task necessitates the creation of an integrated system for irrigation, drainage, and electricity generation, along with scientifically informed agricultural planning that aligns with population distribution in a coordinated manner and serves the interests of the Mushtarak communities and national security requirements. A socialist agricultural system in Iraq could serve as the backbone of the country's economy, providing a reliable source of food and raw materials for national industries.

Such a system is linked to solving the housing problem and providing advanced civil conditions for rural and small-town populations, all addressed within a comprehensive program of economic, population, and educational planning. The small population of Iraq requires high productivity, which can only be achieved through introducing the scientific revolution in all areas of life, updating production methods, and raising the cultural level of the entire society. The link between the industrial, agricultural, and scientific revolutions can double Iraq's productive capabilities with its oil wealth, agricultural resources, and a people thirsty for freedom and progress.

Fourthly, The Kurdish Issue

The Iraqi Communist Party (Central Leadership) addressed the Kurdish issue in Iraq in a number of documents, the latest of which was a study titled 'Two Paths to Solve the Kurdish Issue in Iraq,' which was issued in 1975. This study dealt with the historical and social aspects of the Kurdish issue and outlined the party's policy towards it. This policy can be summarized as considering the Kurds as a distinct nation with the right to determine their own destiny and form their own national state. In 1983, the party believed that the current situation in which the Kurdish people find themselves has made joint struggle between the Kurdish people and the people of every country where the Kurds exist in one state a necessary path to achieve the legitimate national rights of the Kurdish people. For this reason, the party believes that the joint struggle of the Arab and Kurdish peoples in Iraq against imperialism and reaction serves the interests of both peoples and serves their common cause in national liberation, democracy, and social progress. The party affirms the right of the Kurdish people in Iraq to enjoy self-rule within a democratic Iraqi state that recognizes their legitimate national rights and removes all remnants of chauvinistic discrimination against the Kurds, provides all the requirements for the development of Kurdish culture, and compensates them for the persecution, displacement, and destruction they have suffered.

The *Al-Mushtarak* system provides a suitable framework for resolving the Kurdish issue in Iraq, which ensures recognition of the Kurdish people's right to self-determination and enjoyment of their democratic rights, progress, and prosperity. Since the *Al-Mushtarak* system is based on self-governing political-administrative units in geographically or ethnically cohesive areas, its implementation in Iraqi Kurdistan will guarantee the preservation of the Kurdish people's national identity, development of their national culture, and enjoyment of all democratic freedoms. Our party believes that the establishment of the *Al-Mushtarak* system in Iraq should be coupled with the unification of the Kurdish region in Iraq into one political-administrative unit that includes all components in Kurdistan. The vast area of the Kurdish region in Iraq and the geographic diversity of its various parts require the establishment of more than one *Mushtarak* unit that corresponds to the desire and ambition of each part of the Kurdish region in Iraq and the

Kurdish people's desire to govern themselves. Based on these considerations, our party advocates for the unification of the Kurdish region in Iraq into one region called the Kurdistan Region.

The term 'province' means a large autonomous administrative and political unit that includes a number of governorates or districts within the framework of the Iraqi state, similar to the situation in the United States or other similar countries. The province enjoys broad powers for self-governance within its region and participates through elected representatives from the public in the central authority of the state and in all higher bodies. The special administrative status of the Kurdistan region is required by the unique circumstances of the Kurdish people in Iraq and their desire for self-rule. This is in the interest of the joint struggle against imperialism, and in order to establish a democratic system throughout the Iraqi state and secure popular solidarity towards a socialist society.

What applies to the *Al-Mushtarak* system in other parts of Iraq also applies to the Kurdistan region, where representatives elected by the Kurdish *Mushtarak* communities form a council for the region with all the powers of self-governance.

FIFTHLY, ARAB SOLIDARITY

Arab nationalist slogans have been exploited to the extent that the popular masses no longer take them seriously. This is particularly evident when declarations promoting immediate Arab unity and the liberation of Palestine are quickly replaced by collaborative regimes waging war against the Iranian people, as seen during the 1980 Iraq-Iran war. Furthermore, figures linked to imperialism like Saddam Hussein and King Hussein of Jordan, who trade on Arab nationalism, end up dominating the political landscape.

All this occurs while the Zionist flag is being raised in Cairo and the Golan Heights are being openly annexed before the eyes of the world, while preparations are underway to slaughter the Palestinian resistance and bring it to the table of international bargaining.

The enormity of imperialist interests in this region of the world has pushed towards the rise of ruling systems that find their interests in subjugating the Arab peoples and dispersing their national energies, making them incapable of resisting imperialist projects, Zionist aggression, and continuous looting of oil wealth.

Moreover, the situation has been complicated by the presence of political tendencies whose appearance shows a keenness on national interests, while their reality serves imperialist influence. Arab unity has been portrayed as if it could be achieved on the same basis as the national units in some Western European countries such as Germany and Italy. The truth of the matter is that the representatives of these nationalistic tendencies among the Arabs came from the bourgeois and bureaucratic circles who had lost their positions in the previous Ottoman state and turned to control the new systems in the Arab countries established by Western colonial forces, under the cover of nationalist slogans. It is well known that many of those who built or adopted Arab bourgeois nationalistic movements were among those who participated in non-Arab nationalist movements, such as the Turkish movement, or those who were influenced by missionary schools. Therefore, many retrograde and chauvinistic tendencies are associated with these directions.

And thus, many of the regressive and chauvinistic elements, as well as openly traitorous clients like Michel Aflaq and his cohorts, became associated with these movements. Some Arab youth from influential backgrounds also joined these movements, seeing in them and their Western support opportunities to climb the ranks of power. Meanwhile, others were deceived by slogans and fell into working within these movements, believing that they would achieve legitimate liberation aspirations for the Arab people.

The nationalist movements ignored the fundamental differences between the social formations of Islamic countries and the European societies in which the modern bourgeois nationalist trend emerged. In the latter, the nationalist movement expressed the interests of a bourgeois class that had emerged in isolated commercial cities under the rule of a fragmented feudal authority. The movement then evolved in alliance with absolute monarchies. The interests of developing European bourgeoisies were associated with the trend towards a unified market in the countries that spoke a common language because it ensured that the bourgeoisie could surpass their narrow limits by leaving the city for the nation and removing the feudal barriers to capitalist development. This meant, on the one hand, the creation of a national unity that included every nation in Europe, and on the other hand, a bitter struggle between nations over markets and raw materials. European nationalism thus emerged as a chauvinistic, racist nationalist trend that carried with it the effects of capitalist competition, which extended beyond Europe in pursuit of colonies. The nationalist movement became a useful tool in the hands of imperialist bourgeoisies to mislead their people, corrupt their working classes, and justify the colonial subjugation of other peoples.

Such situations have not appeared in Arab countries with long histories of civilization and unique social formations. The modern Arab bourgeoisie did not form as a result of inherited social patterns, but emerged on the margins of Western capitalist expansion and the development of the modern global market. This bourgeoisie was formed bureaucratically and regionally, making it the biggest enemy of Arab national unity, as it saw unity as a threat to its regional interests, which were formed within the context of competition with stronger regional bourgeoisies. However, despite this, it found a useful tool for deception and gaining Western imperial support in nationalist slogans, in opposition to popular movements of the working class. Needless to say, such trading in slogans has alienated Arab masses from these movements and has harmed the cause of Arab popular solidarity due to the deception and political hypocrisy and deals with imperialism that it has engendered.

In addition to these situations, global imperialism, which has dominated the world since at least the last century, has not allowed for the development of an Arab national bourgeoisie that would find its interest in unifying the national market, as happened in Europe in the nineteenth century. Moreover, the bourgeoisie that emerged in the conditions of imperialism in Arab countries was inherently parasitic and disconnected from the production process and the market, which was a significant factor in hindering the growth of industrial bourgeoisie. For these reasons, the Arab bourgeoisie, in general, has been characterized by hostility to any genuine popular unity among Arabs and to any democratic aspirations of the masses.

On the other hand, the working classes in Arab countries have been struggling for democracy and national liberation since their emergence.

As a revolutionary class, they realize that their own liberation cannot be achieved without the liberation of all oppressed sections of society. They are connected to the latest productive forces and do not pursue narrow class interests like the bureaucratic bourgeoisie in power. The working class is the rising social force whose interest lies in national liberation and in achieving Arab democratic unity based on the will of the free masses. This was evident in the early stage of the formation of Arab Communist parties in the 1930s when they gathered in 1935 and called for an Arab democratic union. They struggled with all their energy to defend the Palestinian people and fight Zionism, imperialism, and the puppet governments set up by Western interests.

Despite the emergence of a distorting tendency within the Communist movement, true Arab Communists have been and continue to be at the forefront of the struggle against imperialism, Zionism, and reaction.

The call for bourgeois nationalist thought represents, at present, a significant historical regression for Arabs, dating back to pre-Islamic times of fragmentation and loss. Islam surpassed narrow nationalist thought and considered piety (*taqwa*) as the basis for differentiation between all people, rather than national belonging to this or that nation. The later development of Islamic civilization in the third and fourth centuries of the Hijra opened up broad horizons for cooperation between peoples and called for a universal unity based on cooperation, brotherhood, and equality between nations—a call that European capitalist development did not know, despite its appearance in an advanced era of history. We don't need to look far to see this; we can refer to the literature of Al-Jahiz, the Ikhwān al-Ṣafā, Abū Ḥayyān al-Tawḥīdī, and others to see the advancement of their ideas over those of bourgeois Arab nationalist advocates in modern times, as well as advocates of any bourgeois nationalism in the world today.

For all of these reasons, the call for Arab peoples' solidarity against imperialism, Zionism, and retrogression finds its greatest representatives and strongest social support in the working class. For this call to bear fruit and be a source of strength for Arab peoples in their national struggle, it must be linked to a call for wide-ranging democracy. The Al-Mushtarak system is the framework that can achieve Arab peoples' solidarity based on democracy and the popular will, and harness their energies to be effective and capable of countering imperialist projects and ending the Zionist and retrogressive presence. The forms of this solidarity will undoubtedly be decided through the national democratic struggle.

The Palestinian issue represents the major front in the Arab national liberation struggle against imperialism and Zionism, as the Zionist occupation of Palestine is an extension of Western colonial expansion at the expense of Arab peoples. British imperialism created the Zionist movement as a tool to impose its control over Arab lands, and the Zionist occupation of Palestine serves as a base to strike at the Arab national liberation movement and block any nationalist aspirations of Arab peoples against foreign imperialist control.

Al-Mushtarak calls for Arab solidarity in support of the Palestinian people in their battle to regain their occupied homeland and establish a democratic state, and to stop any attempts by reactionary regimes to slaughter the Palestinian people or threaten the Palestinian resistance into submission at the negotiating table or impose guardianship over the Palestinian people.

The struggle for the liberation of Palestine is not limited to the Palestinian people alone, but rather it passes through the overthrow of Arab puppet regimes and the establishment of democratic systems that open the way for the advancement of Arab peoples, unleash the potential of the masses, and liberate their occupied territories.

APPENDICES

I. MAIN HISTORICAL EVENTS RELATED TO AL-MUSHTARAK STUDY

MAIN EVENTS	AH DATES	CE DATES
CIVILIZED SOCIETIES IN YEMEN, THAMUD, AND COMMERCIAL CITIES LIKE PETRA, AL-HUDAYDAH, AND OTHER CITIES IN TIHAMA	BEFORE 1 AH	BEFORE 622 CE
BIRTH OF PROPHET MUHAMMAD	N/A	570 CE
DEATH OF PROPHET MUHAMMAD	11 AH	632 CE
CALIPH ABU BAKR	11-13 AH	632-634 CE
CALIPH UMAR IBN AL-KHATTAB	13-23 AH	634-644 CE
CALIPH UTHMAN IBN AFFAN	23-35 AH	644-656 CE
CALIPH ALI IBN ABI TALIB	35-40 AH	656-661 CE
UMAYYAD CALIPHATE	41-132 AH	661-750 CE
ZIYAD BIN ABI SUFYAN APPOINTED GOVERNOR OF BASRA	45 AH	665 CE
BATTLE OF KARBALA AND THE MARTYRDOM OF IMAM HUSSAIN	61 AH	680 CE
AL-HAJJAJ BIN YUSUF APPOINTED GOVERNOR OF IRAQ	75 AH	694 CE
ABBASID CALIPHATE	132-656 AH	750-1258 CE
BABAK KHORRAMDIN MOVEMENT	201-222 AH	816-837 CE
ZANJ REBELLION	255-270 AH	869-883 CE
QARMATIAN MOVEMENT	286-372 AH	899-983 CE
BRETHREN OF PURITY (IKHWAN AL-SAFA)	4th CENTURY AH	10th CENTURY CE

Main Events	AH Dates	CE Dates
Abu al-Ala al-Ma'arri	363-449 AH	973-1057 CE
Al-Biruni	362-440 AH	973-1048 CE
Ibn Rushd (Averroes)	520-595 AH	1126-1198 CE
Ibn Khaldun	732-808 AH	1332-1406 CE
Crusades Campaigns (Various periods)	492-690 AH	1095-1291 CE
Conquest of Baghdad by the Mongols	656 AH	1258 CE
Rule of Al-Andalus (Islamic Spain)	92-897 AH	711-1492 CE

II. CHRONOLOGY OF THE SPLIT IN THE IRAQI COMMUNIST PARTY

AFTERMATH OF THE 1958 REVOLUTION AGAINST THE PRO-WESTERN MONARCHY

— SALAM ADEL (CPI General Secretary) and JAMAL HAIDARI (Political Bureau member) advocated for an Iraqi Communist Party takeover of the country, a stance opposed by Soviet leader Khrushchev, who was pursuing a policy of appeasement with the US.

— SALAM ADEL was sent to Moscow for 're-education' while a right-wing leadership took over.

— SALAM ADEL returned from Moscow in late 1962 but did not have enough time to correct the policy of appeasement.

1963

— A US-British instigated coup by Ba'th fascist forces resulted in thousands killed and hundreds of thousands arrested.

— Those killed under torture included SALAM ADEL and JAMAL HAIDARI.

— Many communist cadres who survived felt the party's inability to prevent the coup was due to its policy of appeasement.

FORMATION OF THE 'REVOLUTIONARY CADRES' (AL-KADER AL-THOURAY)

— This line started forming inside the CPI from 1963, gaining momentum when the right-wing leadership advocated in August 1964 to dissolve the CPI and join the new nationalist government party, supported by Moscow.

— This line was led by IBRAHIM ALLAWI and KHALID AHMED ZAKI (Zaki had been a secretary to Bertrand Russell before returning to Iraq).

17 AUGUST 1967

— The CPI split, with the Revolutionary Cadres initially hesitating but eventually deciding to join the larger Central Command Faction, and eventually leading it.

— ZAKI started a peasant uprising in the marshes of the South and was martyred.

— IBRAHIM ALLAWI was elected to the leadership of the powerful Iraqi Engineer's Union.

— The Central Command won the election for the large Iraqi Students Union, initiating a new revolutionary tide.

— The Ba'th Party, led by SADDAM HUSSEIN, took power again in 1968 with help from Western-backed officers and started a new campaign against the Central Command, imprisoning hundreds of its cadres.

— IBRAHIM ALLAWI moved to the party bases in the mountains of Kurdistan-Iraq to continue the political and armed struggle after Saddam Hussein issued a death warrant on him as part of a concerted repression campaign towards the Central Command faction.

— The right-wing Central Leadership faction of the CPI was recognized by the Saddam regime and entered into a coalition with it, supported by Moscow.

Image 2.1. Art by Dia Al-Azzawi. *Az Gou*.

www.ingramcontent.com/pod-product-compliance
Ingram Content Group UK Ltd.
Pitfield, Milton Keynes, MK11 3LW, UK
UKHW041822110325
456069UK00002B/211